KE

LET'S TAKE OUR JOB BACK

www.letstakeourjobback.com

LET'S TAKE OUR JOB BACK

ISBN: 978-0-9952347-9-6

Edited by: Joy-Lynn Stickel, Scott Thomas, Phyllis DayChief, Gloria Roth, and Heidi Brotherston

Cover design: Heidi Brotherston

Book Website
www.letstakeourjobback.com

I dedicate this book to my children,
Carson and Shayla, Kahl and Laurel, Keenan and Lisa,
Shandeah, Kai, and Avery.
You are my world and I love you all so very much

Table of Contents

INTRODUCTION

I nervously walked out onto the stage. The lights blinded my eyes so that I could barely see the silhouettes of the roaring crowd. At least, that's how I pictured them in my mind. In actuality, the 150 impatient students scattered throughout the gymnasium whispered to each other to pass the time as we took our positions on the stage. This was my moment. My life dream. All of my 14 years of it had led up to this. I was going to be a rockstar.

Or not.

As we broke into a loud and gruesomely terrible rendition of "Bad Moon Rising" and "Sultens of Swing," the crowd sat there, many staring at us with blank faces—some laughing. A few of our closest friends were trying their best to cheer us on and rally the rest to do the same. The truth? We were horrible. The songs were barely recognizable.

It's remarkable that anyone who has ever sat through a junior high or high school Battle of the Bands still listens to music at all. The experience is traumatic. The music, if you can call it that, is nearly intolerable to sit through. Yet, the audience doesn't give up on music. They don't stop listening to The Dire Straits or CCR because we made their songs sound terrible. They know full well where the fault lies. We were hacks. Our interpretation of a song doesn't diminish the composition, the composer, or the original artist. Mark Knopfler isn't to blame because we butchered his song. The fault was ours and ours alone.

When it comes to the Christian faith, people regularly blame the Composer when some wannabe hacks play the wrong tune.

Jesus, in all of His perfection, composed a beautiful concerto. He called it Ekklesia. We know it as the church. He orchestrated this melody to become the hope of the world. But the church, with all of her flaws, doesn't always get the tune right. Sometimes, we don't even play the same melody at all. The problem is that people often blame the composer when we play the tune off-key. Many have walked away from faith altogether, deconstructing their relationship with Jesus, all because the church, or people calling themselves Christians, don't play the song the way Jesus intended it to be played.

I love the church! I need to say that because what you are about to read could come across as critical of her, even deconstructionist. My goal is not to deconstruct your faith. I intend to do the opposite.

If you are like me, you have had a lot of frustrations, disappointments, and flat-out angst surrounding the church, especially as of late. Is the Ekklesia operating as Jesus intended? Have we played our own song for so long that we no longer know the original melody? Are we even in the same key? Are we so far gone that we will never recover the beautiful, original tune again?

Let's take a journey together to rediscover the original score Jesus composed. At one time, it was beautifully irresistible to all who heard it. We will not interpret the melody on our own. I am terrified of the consequences of creating yet another off-key version that will cause people to walk away from Jesus and His church. Therefore, we will journey through the scriptures, distinguishing its glorious sound. We will tie together the original score with the early church's interpretation of it. After all, they heard the original melody taught by the Master Himself, so we can confidently assume they played it closest to its original intent. Indeed, their results proved this assumption.

Thousands of books have been written on church history, attempting to interpret its dichromatic past. Many of them are great. Some are not. How will this book be different? Most of the commentaries on the scriptures and the books I have read on church history are focused on what early Christians believed, namely their theology and doctrines. This is NOT one of those books. Instead of focusing just on theology, I want to focus on what Jesus instructed the church to do and how the early church interpreted those instructions. We know what the early church believed, but do we know what they did?

I was stunned when I discovered the early church's daily behaviors, practices and habits. I thought I understood what Jesus taught us to do. I thought I knew how to interpret the original tune, but I discovered I wasn't even playing in the same key. I played major notes where Jesus intended minors and minor notes where He intended majors.

The church, particularly in the first three centuries, played the tune most accurately, and the piece was stunning. But over time, the tune became weaker. There are moments in history where the tune would be beautifully recaptured, resulting in revival and reformation. We will journey through church history to see if we can discern when the melody was played right and when it was not. Our purpose in this journey is to learn how to play the song according to its original purpose and avoid playing it off-key.

Sir Winston Churchill once said, "Those who fail to learn from history are doomed to repeat it."

This book is an invitation to begin the journey with me through history as we attempt to rediscover the original melody Jesus composed. I'm not promising we will uncover it perfectly, but we will endeavor to glean the original score in all its majesty. What if what we uncover is so beautiful that the world would find the church irresistible again? What if what we discover will help us fall in love with her again, too?

CHAPTER ONE

THE STATE OF THE UNION

Our world is in chaos. That is hardly breaking news. Although this is not the first time humanity has faced a crisis, the events between 2020 and 2022 were unique.

THE CHURCH'S RESPONSE TO COVID-19

On March 11, 2020, the World Health Organization declared the Coronavirus a global pandemic. They reported that there were 118,000 cases worldwide, with more than 4,000 deaths, and that the virus had found a foothold on every continent except for Antarctica.[1] Globally, everything came to a screeching halt. Never before had the entire world shut down. Everyone was confused, nervous, and trying to adjust to the 'new normal.' For the first time in history, all of humanity was in the same storm.

At the beginning of the pandemic, most churches were prohibited from meeting in person. Christians were not allowed to assemble. Like many other churches, the one I led moved all of our ministries online and did our best to maintain personal connections with our people by phone or Zoom. Many parishioners were confused, discouraged, and afraid. What we all craved the most was each other. As pastors, we did our best to bring encouragement and strength to our attendees, but it felt like a losing battle. It was just too difficult to make a meaningful connection through a screen. On top of it all, as leaders, we were just as discouraged, confused and afraid as everyone else. It was a trying time.

During the initial lockdown, I was invited to join a group of pastors on a Zoom call. At first, I was excited to see such unity and to gather with over 180 pastors from multiple denominations. However, my excitement was short-lived. While those who organized the gathering intended the call to be encouraging and unifying, the meeting quickly turned political and angry. Pastor after pastor vented their frustration toward the government. The original agenda seemed to get hijacked by a new agenda to lobby the government for the right to gather in large crowds.

I felt torn. As a Canadian citizen, I didn't disagree with the fact that we had the right to assemble, and I could agree that people's mental and spiritual health was being affected by the restrictions to gather. But at the same time, were we willing to put individuals at risk for the right to assemble? The gates of hell couldn't prevail against the church, but the government had the power to shut us down? Had we allowed Christianity to be reduced to a weekly gathering? Were we just a social club? Are we so weak that not being allowed to gather in large crowds for a few weeks could end us?

Was this the church Jesus intended?

This event left me contemplative and introspective. Something inside of me knew I wasn't playing the right melody. The church I would pastor in the future would have to look different than the church I pastor now.

Scottish theologian Henry Drummond said, "It is because to large masses of people Christianity has become synonymous with a

Temple service that other large masses of people decline to touch it."[2] He wrote these words in 1893. And here we are, 130 years later, and we have still made Christianity synonymous with a weekly event.

Let me rephrase that: I have made the church mostly about a weekly event. Our identity, budget, staff, and focus have been allocated toward the Sunday services. When those were restricted, I realized that the Church is so much more than a weekly social gathering. Our Sunday-centric focus was not the original melody Jesus wrote for the Church to play.

THE CHURCH'S RESPONSE TO THE RACIAL TENSIONS

As if the COVID lockdowns weren't enough of a crisis, on May 25, 2020, George Floyd was murdered by Derek Chauvin, a white police officer, in Minneapolis, Minnesota. The world was shocked to see video evidence of Chauvin kneeling on Floyd's neck for over 9 minutes after arresting him on suspicion of using a counterfeit $20 bill. The public outcry was extraordinary.

Mass protests demanding justice for Floyd, along with demonstrations against police brutality in their own countries, took place in over 2,000 cities in the US and around the world, including New York City, Los Angeles, Chicago, Toronto, Mashhad, Milan; Columbus, Ohio; Denver; Des Moines; Houston; Louisville; Memphis; Charlotte, North Carolina; Oakland; Portland, Oregon; San Jose; Seattle; Boston; outside the White House in Washington; outside Chauvin's summer home in Windermere, Florida; and in many other locations. On May 30, 12 states in the U.S. called in the National Guard, and at least 12 major cities imposed curfews that weekend. By June 14, protests had extended into a third week after Floyd's murder in many cities, accompanied by calls to reform and defund police departments throughout the United States.[3]

How did the church respond?

The church was just as divided as the rest of the world. Some pastors promoted Black Lives Matter and protested from their pulpits and on social media. Others were outspoken against both the protests and the Black Lives Matter organization in particular. The research group Barna released a poll that stated that around a third of 400 pastors they surveyed believed that the church should not be involved in movements aimed at political change. The survey claimed that 61% of those who responded said that conversations about race are "too political."[4]

Why such a divide? Why can't we agree on what tune we should be playing, especially in times of crisis and when the world needs us the most?

THE CHURCH'S RESPONSE TO POLITICS

Shortly after all of this surfaced, and while the world was still dealing with COVID, the very controversial 2020 presidential election began in the United States. The church stepped to the forefront, becoming very vocal on both sides. Pastors went public with their views, even using their pulpits to preach their political perspectives as moral and spiritual obligations.

Immediately following the election, the New York Times reported that "Pastors at these churches have preached about fraudulent votes and vague claims of election meddling. They have opened their church doors to speakers promoting discredited theories about overturning President Biden's victory and lent a veneer of spiritual authority to activists who often wrap themselves in the language of Christian righteousness. For these church leaders, Mr. Trump's narrative of the 2020 election has become a prominent strain in an apocalyptic vision of the left running amok."[5]

Even the world noticed that the tune the church was playing was off-key. Those on the extremes of left and right were criticized for being too politically outspoken, and those who were silent were criticized for not speaking up for righteousness.

We were all left asking, what is our place in this world? What are we to do?

On January 6, 2021, riots broke out at the Capitol Buildings in Washington, D.C. Again, the church was thrust to the forefront of the controversy. A Global News article articulated the divide in the church, stating, "The rioters who breached the Capitol on Jan. 6, leading to federal charges against more than 130 people so far, included several people carrying signs with Christian messages, and video showed one man in a fur hat and horns leading others in a prayer inside the Senate chamber."[6]

Later on, in the same article, they quoted Russell Moore, President of the Public Policy Arm of the Southern Baptist Convention, who said that when he saw a "Jesus Saves" sign displayed near a gallows built by rioters, "I was enraged to a degree that I haven't been enraged in memory. This is not only dangerous and unpatriotic but also blasphemous, presenting a picture of the gospel of Jesus Christ that isn't the gospel and is instead its exact reverse."[7]

A year later, Russell Moore would speak out again in his article for Christianity Today. He said, "A year has passed since the January 6 insurrectionist attack on the United States Capitol, and two images still haunt my mind. One is that of a makeshift gallows constructed to threaten the murder of the vice president of the United States. And the other is that of a sign, held above that angry crowd, that read, "Jesus Saves." That these two images can coexist in the same mob is a sign of crisis for American evangelicalism…Such is the sign not of a post-Christian culture but of a post-Christian Christianity, not of a secularizing society but of a paganizing church."[8]

What have we become? And why is the church so polarized? What are we fighting for?

Dr. Gerald Sittser, professor of theology at Whitworth University, answered my questions. He said in his book *Resilient Faith*, "With the accession of Constantine to the throne of the

Roman Empire in 312, the status of Christianity was forever changed. He set in motion a long process that led, first, to the legalization of Christianity in the Roman Empire; then, under the emperor Theodosius, to the official establishment of Christianity as the religion of the empire; and finally, during the Middle Ages, to Christianity's overwhelming cultural dominance over the empire."[9]

He called this dominance Christendom. Then, he offered a stern warning.

> As long as Christians assume we are still living under the old arrangement of Christendom, the church will continue to decline in the West, no matter how ferociously Christians fight to maintain power and privilege. If anything, the harder Christians fight, the more precipitous the decline will be, for cultural power and privilege will come at an increasingly high price. Christians will either accommodate until the faith becomes almost unrecognizable, or they will isolate until their faith becomes virtually invisible.[10]

Shortly after I read Dr. Sittser's book, I came across a statement on Twitter by @RevDaniel. He wrote, "Christianity was never supposed to be about dominating society, but uplifting it — and you can't lift if you're already on top. When Christians cry about losing their freedom, they are really crying over losing their dominance. They want to be Caesar's Empire, not God's Kingdom. People have not turned away from Christ. They have turned away from a religion that worships the idols of political and economic power, slapped a cross on it and tossed the Gospel of Jesus aside, along with its demand for justice, reconciliation and service to the most powerless."

THE RESIDENTIAL SCHOOLS

Speaking of dominance and the abuse of power, on June 30,

2021, the Associated Press made public a report about the residential schools in Canada. "Nearly three-quarters of the 130 residential schools were run by Roman Catholic missionary congregations, with others operated by the Presbyterian, Anglican and the United Church of Canada, which today is the largest Protestant denomination in the country. The Canadian government has acknowledged that physical and sexual abuse was rampant in the schools, with students beaten for speaking their native languages. Last week, the Cowessess First Nation, located about 85 miles (135 kilometers) east of the Saskatchewan capital of Regina, said investigators found "at least 600" unmarked graves at the site of a former Marieval Indian Residential School. Last month, the remains of 215 children, some as young as 3 years old, were found buried on the site of what was once Canada's largest Indigenous residential school near Kamloops, British Columbia."[11]

The stated purpose of the Indian Residential Schools was to make the Indigenous Peoples of Canada embrace Western values and Christianity (those two sets of beliefs were almost inseparable at the time). In the eyes of many state officials, the agent that could and should bring about such rapid change was the Christian church. [12]

We can all agree that this is far from the original melody Jesus wrote for the church. It is easy to understand why so many people would want to distance themselves from the God of these people. It is horrific, inexcusable, and disgusting. Yet, in our disgust, we find it easy to distance ourselves from these perpetrators of vile religion and thank God that "we are not like them" while at the same time justifying our own off-key tune. At least our melody isn't as bad as theirs, right?

Jesus warned of this self-righteous thinking in Luke 18 when he told the parable of a Pharisee and a tax collector. He concluded this thought with the warning, "For those who exalt themselves will be humbled, and those who humble themselves will be exalted."[13]

Even if our tune is a little off-key, it is still wrong.

FILL IN THE BLANK

As an experiment, I decided to conduct a poll on Facebook. I wanted to see how off-key, people in our area thought we were. I asked people to complete the sentence, Christianity is __________.

I received the following answers (these answers are verbatim to what I received):

- Evil? No Vile. reprehensible. that's the one. Yes.
- Oversimplified
- Ignorant
- unapologetic
- An organization of people that continuously contributes to the oppression and hatred of minority groups. It's an ideology that punishes those that are different and ostracizes them rather than the true evils of the world only to inflate their own egos.
- is for weak-minded people that can't think for themselves. It's also a way to con people out of their money so the preachers can live in mansions.
- in love with Donald Trump
- Long overdue for extinction
- Misused by a majority to preach hate and justify bigotry
- A Cult
- Outdated
- Garbage
- A sham
- Biased
- For the gullible
- CANADIAN CATHOLIC RESIDENTIAL TORTURE SCHOOLS

- This is such hate and division propaganda. What a scumbag thing to post in such times. An invitation to attack one's beliefs. Clearly, this will do nothing but get people riled up and arguing. Just pushing forward one of the world's biggest current problems. Who are any of you to put a label on the belief systems of others?? Religion worldwide is under major attack and this is exactly what pushes it. People need to get a grip of themselves, get down off their high horse and just accept that people can believe whatever they want to. And if you don't agree with it or lack the knowledge to understand it. Then booo hoooo. Pull up your big boy/girl pants and move on.

The following week, I posted another ad and asked people to complete this sentence, Jesus is ________.

I received the following answers:

- still better than Mohamed
- A fairy tale about a zombie that rose from the dead
- Savior
- Don't care
- life, everlasting, a true Father figure, friend, & more Phenomenal than Satan or his fallen demonic Angels and followers
- if Jesus was not the son of God, then does that not make his accomplishments even greater?
- the world's first zombie
- a man
- My savior
- A joke
- The world's greatest magician and con man lol
- Lord
- King

- Good
- Fake
- Not real
- Imaginary
- The manifestation of delusional minds
- My everything

I thought it was interesting to see the contrast between the vile negativity spewed at Christianity and how little of that same venom was directed at Jesus. The most negative reaction people could conjure up about Jesus was claiming that He didn't exist.

I tried one more time. I posted another ad, and this time, I asked people to complete the sentence, The church is ___________. As you might expect, the results were quite negative (again, these are verbatim to the answers I received).

People answered:

- Probably not the best place to find god.
- A group of delusional, blinded people looking for a way to act badly, then "wash" their sins away
- Pathetic
- The church is an institution which served once to answer the unanswerable... resulting over time to become a tyranny of answers to punish all those questioning its legitimacy. There is nothing holy about inquisitions or crusades... or any of the rest of the murderous deeds committed under God's name.
- A place to extort your paycheck by means of brainwashing
- A complete cult
- Deluded
- Corrupted
- a place for brainwashed people to pray to an invisible god. The catholic church is a place for priests to sexually assault

children and get away with it.

- Jesus would disapprove of what has become of Christianity.
- An exclusive club for bullies masquerading as righteous.
- "#Not just four Walls & two sets of Doors it is not Just rows of pews with a palate either, it is outdoor's? On hills or a mountain full of sheep or animals, or a ring full of children."
- Corrupt
- A scam
- The body of Christ
- Predatory
- Full of evil.

With such a contrast in answers between who people perceive Jesus to be and how they describe Christianity and the church, it is obvious that everyone knows that today's Christians, me included, aren't playing the same melody Jesus intended.

So what do we do about it? Do we just give up and walk away? Is it hopeless?

Dr. Gerald Sittser didn't think so. After defining the difference between Christendom and Christianity and warning of the church's decline due to our fixation on Christendom, he said, "The best hours of Western Christianity might be ahead of us, not behind us, assuming we dare to think differently about what it means to be Christian and to live as Christians in a culture that is changing."[14]

I want to dare to think differently. I have to. Don't you?

NEHEMIAH'S EXAMPLE

The first area in which we must think differently is our response to our troubled world. I want to take my cue from Nehemiah and how he responded to the crisis in his time.

In 586 B.C., the Babylonians destroyed Jerusalem and its temple. A remnant of Jews left alive were taken into captivity. Then, in 539

B.C., Babylon fell to the Medes and Persians. Again, a few of the Jewish captives were taken as slaves by the Persians in Susa.

The book of Nehemiah begins in 446 B.C. as Nehemiah hears a report from his homeland on the state of his city, Jerusalem. The report comes back that the city is in ruins. Nehemiah 1:4 says that Nehemiah wept for days over the report.

I have given you a few recent reports regarding the modern church and its impact on the world. I am sure that you, just like me, feel deep angst over the state of the union. I haven't even mentioned the recent scandalous reports of Ravi Zacharias, Carl Lentz, Mark Driscoll, Bill Hybels and others. We can feel the angst in the pit of our stomachs, but when Nehemiah received his city's state of the union address, he wept for days.

What did he do about it? He prayed.

ACCEPT RESPONSIBILITY

Going to God in prayer would seem obvious. You and I should do the same concerning the church and the state of our world. However, Nehemiah didn't pray as I would have. Look at what he said to God.

> Nehemiah 1:5-6 (NASB)
> *Please, Lord God of heaven, the great and awesome God, who keeps the covenant and faithfulness for those who love Him and keep His commandments: let Your ear now be attentive and Your eyes open, to hear the prayer of Your servant which I am praying before You now, day and night, on behalf of the sons of Israel Your servants, confessing the sins of the sons of Israel which we have committed against You; I and my father's house have sinned.*

Nehemiah didn't blame God for abandoning him, and he didn't even cast blame on the kings and kingdoms responsible for the destruction of his city. He accepted the blame, both personally and corporately. He said, "I and my father's house have sinned."

Where you cast blame is also where you assign responsibility. Responsibility is simply the ability to respond. By accepting the blame, Nehemiah also took responsibility for the state of his city, giving himself the ability to respond. He wasn't just saying words that he thought would appease God. He was sincere.

Look at how specific he got in his repentance.

> Nehemiah 1:7-9 (NASB)
> *We have acted very corruptly against You and have not kept the commandments, nor the statutes, nor the ordinances which You commanded Your servant Moses. Remember, please, the word which You commanded Your servant Moses, saying, 'If you are unfaithful, I will scatter you among the peoples; but if you return to Me and keep My commandments and do them, though those of you who have been scattered were in the most remote part of the heavens, I will gather them from there and bring them to the place where I have chosen to have My name dwell.'*

Nehemiah was familiar with the commandments given to Moses, as every Jew was. In traditional Jewish education, students would attend synagogue schools by age six. By around ten years of age, they would have learned and memorized the first five books of the Bible, called the Torah.[15]

Memorizing scripture and living by it are two different things. Nehemiah recognized that while he and his ancestors knew the commandments in the Torah, they had failed to do them. Nehemiah included his shortcomings in his repentance by again accepting responsibility, which gave him the ability to respond.

KNOW YOUR IDENTITY

Accepting responsibility would not be enough. Nehemiah needed courage, too. He was human, just like you and me, so I am sure that once he sincerely accepted responsibility for the state of his city, he must have thought, "Who am I? What difference could I make?" Look at what he prayed next.

> Nehemiah 1:10 (NASB)
> *They are Your servants and Your people whom You redeemed by Your great power and by Your strong hand.*

Nehemiah confessed God's great power and strong hand stretched out toward His chosen people, of whom he was a part.

We can learn much from Nehemiah's response to the crisis in his hometown. He is an excellent example of how to respond to the church and our world being in ruins. First, Nehemiah accepted responsibility, which gave him the ability to respond. Second, Nehemiah anchored himself in his identity, which gave him the courage to respond.

BE THE SOLUTION

Nehemiah's third response to the state of his city was to ask God for an opportunity to *be* the solution.

> Nehemiah 1:11 (NASB)
> *Please, Lord, may Your ear be attentive to the prayer of Your servant and the prayer of Your servants who delight to revere Your name, and please make Your servant successful today and grant him mercy before this man."*

As I began to evaluate my prayer life, I realized that I constantly ask God to provide solutions for the problems that I see. When I look at the state of the church, I ask God to send revival. When I look at the state of my nation, I ask God to heal our land. Regardless of the problem, I cast all of the responsibility on God to respond. Nehemiah didn't wait for God to move. He acknowledged God's sovereign power and asked for the opportunity to be the solution.

After he finished praying, Nehemiah made a simple statement. I love how he closed Chapter 1.

> Nehemiah 1:11 (NASB)
> *Now I was the cupbearer to the king.*

It is meaningful that he concludes the chapter by stating his current position rather than opening with it. It reveals his mind. He wasn't going to allow the fact that he was technically a prisoner of war, a slave, and a mere cupbearer to be an excuse as to why he couldn't make a difference. Excuses release us from our duty or responsibility. I wonder how many times I have made excuses and missed God-given opportunities.

SO WHAT DO WE DO NOW?

We will use Nehemiah's prayer as our template for rediscovering the original tune Jesus composed for the church.

1. **Accept Responsibility.**
   We need to accept personal and corporate responsibility to give ourselves the ability to respond. To take responsibility, we must get specific about how we have "sinned." If we don't know where we have missed the mark, we will likely miss it repeatedly. Defining our sins is not as easy as one would think. Do our current beliefs and traditions define sin in the same way that God defines sin? The answer might surprise you. It surprised me.

In the first section of this book, I will define our responsibility from both the scriptures and by evaluating the practices of the church throughout history.

2. **Know our identity.**
   We must anchor ourselves in our God-given identity to gain the courage to respond. All of us battle insecurity in one form or another, and when we look at the state of the world, it is easy to minimize ourselves and our ability to make a difference.
   In the second section of this book, I want to take a deep dive into our personal and corporate identity, as Jesus defined it. The early church was clear in its identity, allowing them to transform their societies. What if we could do the same?

3. **Be the solution.**
   We need practical plans and strategies to be the solution. Section three will outline Jesus' strategies and how the early church applied them. These strategies were so effective that Roman emperors feared the influence of a few Jewish fishermen from the outskirts of their empire. What if these same strategies would work today? I believe they will. I believe that if the church takes its job back, it will once again become the most influential, irresistible movement on the planet.

It's easy to look at the state of the union of the Western Church, throw up our hands in exasperation and say, "What can we do?" What if I told you the answer is not as complicated as you might think? It's hidden in plain sight in the scriptures. We know it works because the results have been staggering when appropriately applied in church history. I titled this book "Let's Take Our Job Back" because the church once did its job effectively, and we can do it again!

Let's discover the original tune and start playing it again—together.

SECTION ONE

ACCEPT RESPONSIBILITY

CHAPTER TWO
WHO IS TO BLAME?

"I and my father's house have sinned."
~Nehemiah

Blame is defined as assigning responsibility for a fault or wrong. We all blame others for our behaviors, thoughts, or negative feelings. It's not unusual to pass blame to someone else for making us late, making us feel guilty, or making us angry.

Blaming others provides a quick escape from guilt. When we feel defensive, we look for something or someone to blame. If we don't hold ourselves accountable for the consequences of our behaviors, thoughts or feelings, we continue living life clueless that our problems are essentially our fault. Refusing to take personal responsibility strips us of our ability to respond.

Blaming others is an easy out, which makes Nehemiah's prayer even more impressive. Nehemiah didn't have to accept personal responsibility. He was probably not even alive when Babylon destroyed Jerusalem. Yet, he chose to confess his "sin" anyway.

Have you ever thought of examining the sin that Nehemiah was confessing? I hadn't until recently. I assumed the sins he referred to were the common ones, like disobeying the 10 Commandments, sexual immorality, idol worship, etc. Yet, the prophet Isaiah penned something different.

WHAT IS SIN?

Many Bible experts believe that Isaiah 58 was written in 539 B.C. by prophets from the school of Isaiah rather than by the prophet himself. If you remember from our timeline in the book of Nehemiah, this was the time that the Medes and Persians conquered Babylon. The Persian kings were the first to allow some of the Jews to venture back to their homes in Jerusalem.

Isaiah 58 was written to the Jews during this time, and I believe there are direct prophetic references to Nehemiah and his role in rebuilding the city. That makes this chapter so poignant to the definition of the "sins" Nehemiah confessed to God in his prayer in Nehemiah 1.

> Isaiah 58:1 (NLT)
> *"Shout with the voice of a trumpet blast. Shout aloud! Don't be timid. Tell my people Israel of their sins!"*

Here we go. I expect the following verses to be a list of the typical sins. But look how God describes their sin..

> Isaiah 58:2-3 (NLT)
> *Yet they act so pious! They come to the Temple every day and seem delighted to learn all about me. They act like a righteous nation that would never abandon the laws of its God. They ask me to take action on their behalf, pretending they want to be near me. 'We have fasted before you!' they say. 'Why aren't you impressed?*

We have been very hard on ourselves, and you don't even notice it!'

Wait. What? Their list of sins includes going to church every day, acting as a righteous nation, fasting, and pretending that they want to be near God. These are not the sins I was expecting. These wouldn't even make my list of sins.

I admit I felt highly convicted the first time I read this. I still do, as I am rereading this right now. I have made church attendance, prayer, and the righteousness of my nation a significant priority. I joined in meetings with other pastors lobbying the government to allow us to go to church once a week, and here, God wasn't impressed with the Israelites attending church daily.

But how is this sin?

The word sin originates from the Old English term "syn" translated from Biblical Greek and Hebrew, indicating the action of missing the mark. In the original sense of New Testament Greek, "sin" is a failure in hitting the bullseye, primarily in spear-throwing. In Hebrew, hata is the word used for "sin," and this word originates in archery and refers to missing the "gold" at the center of a target but hitting the target.[1]

Sin means to miss the bullseye, but it doesn't necessarily mean missing the target altogether. That is important because in Isaiah 58, God counts their attending the temple daily as a miss, yet later in the chapter, He invites them to "*Keep the Sabbath day holy. Don't pursue your own interests on that day, but enjoy the Sabbath and speak of it with delight as the Lord's holy day. Honor the Sabbath in everything you do on that day, and don't follow your own desires or talk idly.*"[2]

He also counts their fasting as a miss in verse 3.

Isaiah 58-3-5 (NLT)

'We have fasted before you!' they say. 'Why aren't you impressed?

We have been very hard on ourselves, and you don't even notice it!'
"I will tell you why!" I responded. "It's because you are fasting to please yourselves. Even while you fast, you keep oppressing your workers. What good is fasting when you keep on fighting and quarreling? This kind of fasting will never get you anywhere with me. You humble yourselves by going through the motions of penance, bowing your heads like reeds bending in the wind. You dress in burlap and cover yourselves with ashes. Is this what you call fasting? Do you really think this will please the Lord?

To which we all answer, "Yes! Of course, it will please you." Come on, don't act so righteous with me. You have thought, just as I have, that regular church attendance, daily prayer and devotions, bowing your heads and raising your hands in worship, and fasting were all things that impressed God. Right?

Not according to God Himself. According to God, these things are on target, but not the bullseye. So, what is the bullseye?

Isaiah 58:6-7 (NLT)
"No, this is the kind of fasting I want: Free those who are wrongly imprisoned; lighten the burden of those who work for you. Let the oppressed go free, and remove the chains that bind people. Share your food with the hungry, and give shelter to the homeless. Give clothes to those who need them, and do not hide from relatives who need your help.

Ok, now he's getting personal in talking about hiding from relatives who need our help. How is that a type of fasting? According to God, it is. According to God, hitting the bullseye requires justice, treating our employees and co-workers right, helping people get free, feeding the hungry, housing the homeless, and clothing the naked.

Does that sound familiar? It's the exact instructions Jesus gave his disciples in Matthew 25.

> Matthew 25: 34-36
> *"Then the King will say to those on his right, 'Come, you who are blessed by my Father; take your inheritance, the kingdom prepared for you since the creation of the world. For I was hungry and you gave me something to eat, I was thirsty and you gave me something to drink, I was a stranger and you invited me in, I needed clothes and you clothed me, I was sick and you looked after me, I was in prison and you came to visit me.'*

I have realized that I have defined Christianity as a weekly gathering and made my faith a private, personal relationship with God. Yet, God defines Christianity as a public expression that must impact the world around us. I have majored in the minors and have minored in the majors, and just like Nehemiah, I have sinned. I have missed the mark. My very personal faith may be on the target, but it's not the bullseye.

The sins God listed in Isaiah 58 are entitlement, self-righteousness, self-interest, division, abuse, and ignoring the needs around us. When I look at this list, I can easily see how applicable they are to today's church. I don't think you will disagree with me that our modern Christianity often acts entitled and self-righteous, puts our interests above others, is divisive and abusive at times, and seems oblivious to the needs of our communities.

Are we bold enough to confess as Nehemiah did, "I and the church have sinned?"

WHAT IS A CHRISTIAN?

Isaiah 58 was a catalyst scripture for me. It stirred a lot of questions. What if I have misunderstood what it means to be

Christian? What do I need to change? What if the church is missing out on its role and purpose? Could this be why the church is so despised today when it was once irresistible? Are we too far gone that we can never get back on target?

These questions led me to a deep study of the scriptures and research of the early church. I didn't go looking for what to believe. I went looking for what to do. Isaiah 58 indicates that God is looking for more than just a right belief system or a proper expression of worship. He is looking for a faith that makes an impact, not just on us but on the world around us. Did Jesus require the same things?

Yes!

In fact, in His very first public message, commonly known as the Sermon on the Mount, Jesus said,

> Matthew 5:14-16 (NASB)
> *"You are the light of the world. A city set on a hill cannot be hidden; nor do people light a lamp and put it under a basket, but on the lampstand, and it gives light to all who are in the house. Your light must shine before people in such a way that they may see your good works, and glorify your Father who is in heaven."*

Jesus said your light *must* shine before people. This wasn't a suggestion. He expected His followers to impact people. He uses the metaphor of a light on a lampstand to explain how our good works will light a path for people toward God. Christianity isn't a private belief system. It isn't just having a personal faith in God. It's much more than that. As James, the brother of Jesus, would later write, *"You believe that God is one. You do well; the demons also believe, and shudder. But are you willing to acknowledge, you foolish person, that faith without works is useless?"*[3]

You might be asking, "Hold on a minute, we are saved by grace, not works, right?" Absolutely. Salvation is by grace, as Paul said in

Ephesians 2:8, *"For by grace you have been saved through faith; and this is not of yourselves, it is the gift of God."* But Christianity is much more than being saved from our sins.

Salvation is the starting block. It is the beginning of the race. There is still an entire race to run.

THE PROTESTANT REFORMATION

Our modern theology of "salvation is by grace alone and not by our works" originated with the Protestant Reformation spearheaded by Martin Luther in 1517.

In 1515, Pope Leo X granted a plenary indulgence intended to finance the construction of St. Peter's Basilica in Rome.[4] In the teaching of the Catholic Church, an indulgence (Latin: *indulgentia*, from *indulgeo*, 'permit') is "a way to reduce the amount of punishment one has to undergo for sins."[5] The *Catechism of the Catholic Church* describes an indulgence as "a remission before God of the temporal punishment due to sins whose guilt has already been forgiven, which the faithful Christian who is duly disposed gains under certain prescribed conditions through the action of the Church which, as the minister of redemption, dispenses and applies with authority the treasury of the satisfactions of Christ and all of the saints."[6]

The indulgence Pope Leo X granted in 1515 would apply to almost any sin, including adultery and theft. All other indulgence preaching was to cease for the eight years in which it was offered. Indulgence preachers were given strict instructions on how the indulgence was to be preached, and they were much more laudatory of the indulgence than those of earlier indulgences.[7]

Johann Tetzel was commissioned to preach and offer the indulgence in 1517, and his campaign in cities near Wittenberg drew many Wittenbergers to travel to these cities and purchase them since sales had been prohibited in Wittenberg and other Saxon cities.[8]

Being from the area, Luther had a rather negative experience with the indulgences connected to All Saints' Church, Wittenberg. As early as 1514, he had preached against the abuse of indulgences and the way they cheapened grace rather than requiring true repentance. Luther became especially concerned in 1517, when his parishioners, returning from purchasing Tetzel's indulgences, claimed they no longer needed to repent and change their lives to be forgiven of sin. After hearing what Tetzel had said about indulgences in his sermons, Luther began to study the issue more carefully and contacted experts on the subject. He preached about indulgences several times in 1517, explaining that true repentance was better than purchasing an indulgence.[9]

"This one and firm rock, which we call the doctrine of justification," insisted Luther, "is the chief article of the whole Christian doctrine, which comprehends the understanding of all godliness."[10]

During the Protestant Reformation, Lutheran and Calvinist theologians generally believed the Catholic doctrine of the means of grace to be a mixture of reliance upon the grace of God and confidence in the merits of one's own works performed in love. These Reformers argued that salvation is entirely a free gift of God, dispensed by the Holy Spirit according to the redemptive work of Christ alone.[11]

Luther didn't believe that we, as believers, should stop doing works. In fact, in theses 41–47 of the 95 Theses he posted on the door of All Saints Church in Wittenberg, he criticized indulgences because they discouraged works of mercy by those who purchased them. Here, he begins to use the phrase, "Christians are to be taught..." to state how he thinks people should be instructed on the value of indulgences. He believed they should be taught that giving to the poor is incomparably more important than buying indulgences, that buying an indulgence rather than giving to the poor invites God's wrath, and that doing good works makes a person better while buying indulgences does not.[12]

While Luther's Reformation was necessary, we as humans have a predictable tendency to climb from one ditch into another. As the saying goes, "For every mile of road, there are two miles of ditch."

Over the last 500 years, the church has moved beyond Luther's original intent, slowly drifting more and more away from works to the degree that now we have reduced our entire faith to a simple prayer and a personal belief system.

FAITH WITHOUT WORKS IS DEAD

It is true that salvation is by grace alone, but an alive faith also requires works.

> James 1:22-25 (NASB)
> *But prove yourselves doers of the word, and not just hearers who deceive themselves. For if anyone is a hearer of the word and not a doer, he is like a man who looks at his natural face in a mirror; for once he has looked at himself and gone away, he has immediately forgotten what kind of person he was. But one who has looked intently at the perfect law, the law of freedom, and has continued in it, not having become a forgetful hearer but an active doer, this person will be blessed in what he does.*

James indicates that when we activate our faith by being doers, we will grow deeper into it. But what kind of activities is he talking about? He tells us in verse 15.

> James 1:14-17 (NASB)
> *What use is it, my brothers and sisters, if someone says he has faith, but he has no works? Can that faith save him? If a brother or sister is without clothing and in need of daily food, and one of you says to them, "Go in peace, be warmed and be filled," yet*

you do not give them what is necessary for their body, what use is that? In the same way, faith also, if it has no works, is dead, being by itself.

This sounds familiar, doesn't it? Feed the hungry, clothe the naked. Help the helpless. It was what Jesus told His disciples to do in Matthew 25. It's also what the prophets told the Israelites to do in Isaiah 58.

Isaiah 58:10-11 (NLT)
Feed the hungry, and help those in trouble. Then your light will shine out from the darkness, and the darkness around you will be as bright as noon. The Lord will guide you continually, giving you water when you are dry and restoring your strength. You will be like a well-watered garden, like an ever-flowing spring.

In the same manner that Jesus told His followers to be "the light of the world" by doing good deeds, Isaiah says, "Feed the hungry," and then your light will shine.

I love how both Isaiah and Jesus use the metaphor of light shining in the darkness. Darkness is simply the absence of light. It has no power in and of itself. I hear some Christians lament about how dark the world is becoming. If the world is dark, it's because there isn't enough light, and according to Jesus, we are the light. Is it possible that the reason the world has become darker is that we, as the church, have ceased our responsibilities and have reduced our faith to a personal belief system? Jesus warned His followers in Matthew 5 not to put the light "under a basket." Is it possible that the basket he is referring to is the church? Have we reduced the church to a weekly gathering in a building?

We may be bold enough to shine our light at a weekly gathering in a building called the church, but the light was not meant to be hidden there. It was meant to be a "city on a hill" that "cannot be hidden." We cannot invite the darkness under our basket and expect it to be dispelled in the streets. The light must go to where the darkness is to have any effect.

The devil doesn't mind a Christian attending church and keeping his or her faith private and personal. What makes him quake in his shoes is a Christian who does "good deeds before men" because that is when the darkness is dispelled and people find their way to God.

I and my fathers have sinned. I was raised in the church and have been taught its traditions, doctrines, and best practices. I have missed the mark by reducing my faith to a view instead of helping you. I have hidden my light under the basket of a weekly gathering instead of creating a movement in my city.

The church was never meant to be a location or a weekly gathering. It was always intended to be a movement. In fact, the word church isn't even in the Bible. That's the wrong interpretation.

WHAT IS THE CHURCH?

There is an old Italian proverb, '*Traduttore, traditore*' – which means "the translator is a traitor" or "to translate is to betray." The improper translation of "church" in our Bibles proves this proverb true. We have been subtly betrayed.

The term church is a derivative of the German word Kirche, which means "house of the Lord" or "temple." The word *Kirche* or "church" in English was used to interpret, rather than translate, the Greek word *ekklesia* throughout most of the New Testament. Ekklesia means "called out ones" or, more accurately, "*a socio-political gathering of citizens who were called together to attend to the concerns of their city.*"[13]

The difference between the two interpretations of the word Jesus used in Matthew 16:18 is stark. *Church* refers to a static institution that functions in buildings for members to go to on specific occasions, whereas *Ekklesia* refers to an uncontrollable, building-less people movement designed to operate 24/7 in the marketplace for the purpose of having an impact on everybody and everything.[14] So which is it? What did Jesus say He would build?

In 1522, William Tyndale began translating the Greek New Testament into English. You would think translating the Bible into the people's language would be welcomed, right? Well, not exactly. This seemingly innocent act would cost Tyndale his life.

His translations were viewed as a threat to the church. The most significant controversy came when Tyndale translated the Greek word ekklesia as *congregation* rather than *church*.[15] It has been asserted this translation choice "was a direct threat to the Church's ancient – but so Tyndale here made clear, non-scriptural – claim to be the body of Christ on earth. To change these words was to strip the Church hierarchy of its pretensions to be Christ's terrestrial representative, and to award this honor to individual worshipers who made up each congregation."[16]

In other words, the church and government leaders felt like their authority and ability to control the masses was threatened by this interpretation. Organizations are easier to control. But Jesus didn't intend to build an organization. He started a movement.

This simple translation decision has affected our understanding of the church and its purpose on earth. Today, we say we are "going to church," referring to a building, a temple. We go to a building to practice our faith and express our worship to God, but our faith was never meant to be controlled or confined.

For ten years, Tyndale was branded as an outlaw and hunted by the authorities. Eventually, he was betrayed by a friend named Henry Phillips, who turned him over to authorities representing the Holy Roman Empire. He was seized in Antwerp in 1535 and held in the castle of Vilvoorde (Filford) near Brussels.[17] Some suspect that Bishop Stokesley hired Phillips to gain Tyndale's confidence and then betray him.

He was tried on a charge of heresy and was found guilty and condemned to be burned to death. Tyndale "was strangled to death while tied at the stake, and then his dead body was burned" on October 6, 1536. His final words, spoken "at the stake with a fervent zeal, and a loud voice," were reported as "Lord! Open the King of England's eyes."[18]

Interestingly enough, four English translations of the Bible were published in England at the king's command within four years of Tyndale's death. All were based on his work. Then, less than one hundred years later, King James released his "authorized" version of the Bible in which Tyndale's words accounted for 84% of the New Testament and for 75.8% of the Old Testament books that he translated."[19]

Despite King James using most of Tyndale's translation, he still insisted on using the word "church" instead of the proper term, ekklesia. Why? Ed Silvosa explains his intentions this way:

> The Anglican Church, of which King James was the head, was one of the main vehicles through which he channeled his royal authority. He did it through its episcopal form of government, implementing his rule through the bishops he appointed. The notion that common folks could have an authoritative voice in religious matters constituted a real and present threat to him. To counter this, King James convened 47 scholars to produce a new version of the Bible that eventually became known as the King James "Authorized" Version.
>
> Granted, new versions usually improve on previous ones, and this one was no exception—except that at the very outset King James placed fifteen directives on the scholars in charge of the project. One of those directives specifically prohibited them from translating the Greek word ekklesia as assembly because

> it went counter to the Anglican Church's episcopal form of government. Instead, a different word was to be used: church. Clearly, King James's intention was to keep the government of the Church in his hands.[20]

So, you see. The translators have betrayed us. Yet, despite their best attempts to control the organization, Jesus was right when He said, "I will build my *ekklesia* (called out ones), and the gates of hell will not prevail against it." The movement is still alive and well. Hell will not hold her back.

Does understanding the proper translation mean we give up gathering in buildings? No! Absolutely not.

> Hebrews 10:19-25
> *Therefore, brothers and sisters, since we have confidence to enter the Most Holy Place by the blood of Jesus, by a new and living way opened for us through the curtain, that is, his body, and since we have a great priest over the house of God, let us draw near to God with a sincere heart and with the full assurance that faith brings, having our hearts sprinkled to cleanse us from a guilty conscience and having our bodies washed with pure water. Let us hold unswervingly to the hope we profess, for he who promised is faithful. And let us consider how we may spur one another on toward love and good deeds, not giving up meeting together, as some are in the habit of doing, but encouraging one another—and all the more as you see the Day approaching.*

The writer of Hebrews says we can have confidence and anchor our faith in our relationship with God because of Jesus. A new way has been opened for us. The veil has been torn, and we can have full confidence in our relationship with Him, regardless of the location. We don't need to go to a temple anymore to find God. He is with us, always. But, still, the writer of Hebrews says we should gather together as God's "called out ones," a people meeting for a purpose. Why? So that we can encourage and strengthen one another "toward love and good deeds." There it is again. Good deeds.

Isaiah 58 rebuked the Israelites for going to the temple daily but then closed the chapter this way.

> Isaiah 58:13-14 (NLT)
> *"Keep the Sabbath day holy. Don't pursue your own interests on that day, but enjoy the Sabbath and speak of it with delight as the Lord's holy day. Honor the Sabbath in everything you do on that day, and don't follow your own desires or talk idly. Then the Lord will be your delight. I will give you great honor and satisfy you with the inheritance I promised to your ancestor Jacob. I, the Lord, have spoken!"*

Our weekly gatherings are not about us. It's not about pursuing our own interests, preferences, or needs. It is not about belonging to a static institution. It is not our only opportunity to connect with God. We can connect with Him anytime, anywhere. The church is not about comfort, command, control, or coin. The weekly gatherings are for us to strengthen one another and to be equipped to do the work of the ministry.

WE HAVE MISSED THE MARK

What if we were to take the blame for missing the bullseye in our understanding of what it means to be Christian and what it means to be the church? And what if we were to accept the responsibility for the darkness in our world, recognizing that darkness is simply the absence of light? What if we took the light to our city?

Nehemiah did. And, he was just a cupbearer, a prisoner of war. So did Martin Luther King (MLK).

MLK preached a sermon in 1954 at Dexter Avenue Baptist Church in Montgomery, Alabama, in which he said, "No man should become so involved in his personal ambitions that he forgets that other people exist in the world. Indeed if my life's work is not developed for the good of humanity, it is [meaningless] and Godless."[21]

The prophet in Isaiah 58 said that if we would feed the hungry, clothe the naked, take care of the oppressed, and meet the needs of people (even our demanding relatives), we would be known as the rebuilders of cities and the restorer of homes.

Isaiah 58:12 (NLT)
Some of you will rebuild the deserted ruins of your cities. Then you will be known as a rebuilder of walls and a restorer of homes.

Did the members of the early church practice their faith in this way? Did they have a different understanding of what it means to be a Christian than we do today? Did they keep their faith personal and confined to a temple?

In the next chapter, we will begin studying what the early church did, not just what they believed.

CHAPTER THREE

WHAT DID THE EARLY CHURCH DO?

We are living in uncertain times. That is hardly newsworthy, but it is true. The Covid pandemic affected more than just our health. It left the economic, political, religious and business worlds more vulnerable, more unstable and less predictable. The post-pandemic world has new levels of insecurity and fear, especially in leaders. It is a dangerous but exciting time.

I think it is a crucial time for the church. I believe Christians everywhere need to anchor themselves in the realization that we were made on purpose, for a purpose, for such a time as this. We must recognize that we aren't going back to the way it was and that this is a critical time to re-vision what's ahead.

What will the church of the future look like? We have an opportunity to shape that. What an important and daunting task! How can we be confident that we can get it right?

My good friend and mentor, Leon Fontaine, taught me that foresight is the ability that distinguishes great leaders from leaders who are barely managing. To develop foresight, a leader must become a student of history, an analyst of the present, and a prophet of the future. These three ingredients are essential, and when used in balance, they are powerful.

To know what the future church looks like, we must study the past and learn from what the early church did right and what it did wrong. We must also analyze what is working and not working today by becoming, as Andy Stanley says, "a student rather than a critic." We must also rely on the Holy Spirit to prophetically lead us into the future.

Let's look into the history of the early church. Most of us who have studied church history are more familiar with their theology and doctrines than we are with their day-to-day behaviors. Let's look beyond what they believed. What did the early believers do?

We can find some of their best practices in the scriptures, and I will highlight some of those as we go along, but I want to look at accounts throughout the first three centuries written by the church and about the church, highlighting what they majored in and practiced as believers.

THE FIRST AND SECOND CENTURY

The first account written about the early Christians that we have on record was written by Pliny the Younger (AD 61-113). Pliny was the governor of the important Roman province of Bithynia-Pontus, which in the modern world is in the northern part of Turkey. He was the first public Roman figure to show concern about the new sect growing in his region called Christians. Pliny wrote a letter that we still have today to Emperor Trajan in the year 112.

The letter begins, "It is my custom to refer all my difficulties to you, Sir, for no one is better able to resolve my doubts and to inform my ignorance."[1]

The difficulties Pliny the Younger was referring to was his concern over the economic impact Christianity was having on his region. When people became Christians, they stopped their sacrifices at the pagan temples. This meant they stopped buying the animals for sacrifice and, in some cases, even stopped buying the meat that was taken from the temple sacrifices to be sold in the local markets.

This concern was not unique to the province of Bithynia-Pontus. It was reported by Tertullian (AD 160-225), a former lawyer and leading Christian intellectual from Carthage, that pagans were complaining in his region of Carthage that revenues were down in the temples on account of so many people converting to Christianity as well.[2]

In his letter to Emperor Trajan, Pliny seeks advice on handling the Christians in his region. He wrote, "I do not know the nature or the extent of the punishments usually meted out to them, nor the grounds for starting an investigation and how far it should be pressed." He then reported that "a great many individuals of every age and class, both men and women, are being brought to trial."

He goes on to outline his policy in handling the Christians so far, basically seeking the approval of his emperor, "For the moment, this is the line I have taken with all persons brought before me on the charge of being Christians. I have asked them in person if they are Christians, and if they admit it, I repeat the question a second and third time, with a warning of the punishment awaiting them. If they persist, I order them to be led away for execution; for, whatever the nature of their admission, I am convinced that their stubbornness and unshakeable obstinacy ought not to go unpunished."[3]

Pliny proudly tells the Emperor that he has figured out a way to identify real Christians. He wrote, "I considered that I should dismiss any who denied that they were or ever had been Christians when they had repeated after me a formula of invocation to the gods and had made offerings of wine and incense to your statue, and furthermore had reviled the name of Christ, none of which things, I understand, any genuine Christian can be induced to do."[4]

Here is where it gets interesting. Pliny wants to understand the Christians and, in particular, how they worship. Christianity is new and unknown to the Romans. Christians didn't seem religious in that they didn't dress differently, eat different foods, and build elaborate temples, yet Pliny wanted to know what they believed and what they did. He's not the only one. The emperor was curious, too. So, Pliny reports that he attempted "to extract the truth by torture from two slave-women, whom they call deaconesses."[5]

In particular, Pliny wanted to know about their worship.

> They also declared that the sum total of their guilty or error amounted to no more than this: they had met regularly before dawn on a fixed day to cant verses alternately among themselves in honor of Christ as if to a god, and also to bind themselves by oath, not for any criminal purpose, but to abstain from theft, robbery and adultery, to commit no breach of trust and not to deny a deposit when called upon to restore it. After this ceremony, it had been their custom to disperse and reassemble later to take food of an ordinary, harmless kind.[6]

Pliny discovered, along with the Emperor and all of Rome, that the Christians did three main things: 1) they gathered together to worship Jesus once a week; 2) they were disciplined in their behavior and abstained from any criminal activities; 3) they were incredibly generous and made sure that everyone who came into contact with them was fed and taken care of.

These three behaviors are what the historical church became known for: worshiping Jesus as God, treating people with love and respect, and taking care of the poor.

These activities were hardly criminal and did not deserve persecution or execution, yet Emperor Trajan replied, "You have followed the right course of procedure, my dear Pliny. These people must not be hunted out; if they are brought before you and the charge against them is proved, they must be punished."[7] A year later, Pliny died in the year 113.

IGNATIUS

During the reign of Trajan, a very public arrest and execution of a Christian occurred. Ignatius, bishop of Antioch, was arrested and ordered to stand trial in Rome. During his long journey from Turkey to Rome, he was permitted to write letters to Christians in various communities. Seven of his letters survived.

In his letter to Christians in Ephesus, he wrote, "Pray continually for the rest of humankind as well, that they may find God, for there is in them hope of repentance. Therefore allow them to be instructed by you, at least by your deeds. In response to their anger, be gentle; in response to their boasts, be humble; in response to their slander, offer prayers; in response to their errors, be steadfast in faith; in response to their cruelty, be civilized; do not be eager to imitate them. Let us show by our forbearance that we are their brothers and sisters, and let us be eager imitators of the Lord."[8]

This letter shows the church's response to the unjustified persecution of Christians at this time. They didn't lobby or debate in the Roman Senate about the injustices committed against them. Instead, they responded by following Jesus' command to love their enemies and bless those who persecuted them.

Ignatius was tried and executed in Rome, probably fed to wild beasts in the Colosseum.[9]

NO NEED AMONG THEM

Justin Martyr wrote further details about how Christians worshiped in 150 AD:

> And on the day called Sunday, all who live in cities or in the

> country gather together to one place, and the memoirs of the apostles or the writings of the prophets are read, as long as time permits; then, when the reader has ceased, the president verbally instructs, and exhorts to the imitation of these good things. Then we all rise together and pray, and, as we before said, when our prayer is ended, bread and wine and water are brought, and the president in like manner offers prayers and thanksgiving, according to his ability, and the people assent, saying Amen and there is a distribution to each, and a participation of that over which thanks have been given, and to those who are absent a portion is sent by the deacons. And they who are well to do, and willing, give what each thinks fit; and what is collected is deposited with the president, who succors the orphans and widows, and those who, through sickness or any other cause, are in want, and those who are in bonds, and the strangers sojourning among us, and in a word takes care of all who are in need.[10]

Notice, with a few minor exceptions, the similarities between church worship in 150 AD and today's services. Amazing! The exceptions, of course, are that every service is closed with the focus on taking care of the needs among them. This regular practice sheds a powerful light on what Luke wrote about the first-century church in Acts 2 and 4.

> Acts 2:42-47
> *They devoted themselves to the apostles' teaching and to fellowship, to the breaking of bread and to prayer. Everyone was filled with awe at the many wonders and signs performed by the apostles. All the believers were together and had everything in common. They sold property and possessions to give to anyone who had need. Every day they continued to meet together in the temple*

courts. They broke bread in their homes and ate together with glad and sincere hearts, praising God and enjoying the favor of all the people. And the Lord added to their number daily those who were being saved.

Acts 4:32-35
All the believers were one in heart and mind. No one claimed that any of their possessions was their own, but they shared everything they had. With great power the apostles continued to testify to the resurrection of the Lord Jesus. And God's grace was so powerfully at work in them all that there were no needy persons among them. For from time to time those who owned land or houses sold them, brought the money from the sales and put it at the apostles' feet, and it was distributed to anyone who had need.

We have on record that the three practices of the first-century Christians–worshiping Jesus as God, treating people with love and respect, and taking care of the poor–continued for at least another one hundred years. Did they continue to prioritize caring for each other and the needy beyond that time, even though persecution against them was becoming more and more intense?

THE THIRD CENTURY

Quintus Septimius Florens Tertullian (AD 160-225), a former lawyer and leading Christian intellectual from Carthage, wrote a letter to Scapula (governor of Carthage) in the year 215. Scapula had launched an aggressive and violent campaign against the church. Tertullian wrote in the opening lines of his defense, "We are not in any great perturbation or alarm about the persecutions we suffer from the ignorance of men; for we have attached ourselves to this sect, fully accepting the terms of its covenant…For our religion commands us to love even our enemies, and to pray for those who persecute us, aiming at a perfection all its own. For everyone loves those who love them; it is peculiar to Christians alone to love those who hate them."[11]

Tertullian explained this "peculiar love" in great detail, stating that Christians gave their money for "feeding and burying the poor, for boys and girls destitute of property and parents; and further for old people confined to the house, and victims of shipwreck; and any who are in the mines, who are exiled to an island, or who are in prison merely on account of God's church–these become the wards of their confession."[12]

THE SO-CALLED LETTER TO DIOGNETUS

An ancient document called the So-Called Letter to Diognetus also details the regular practices and behaviors of the early church. Historians aren't certain of the authorship of this amazing document. Although it was once believed to have been penned by Justin the Martyr, it is more commonly believed to have been written somewhere in the second or third centuries. Regardless, it explains the motivation behind the church's extraordinary love and generosity toward a society that so widely persecuted them. The author's reasoning reads like this: "But any man who takes upon his neighbor's load, who is willing to use his superiority to benefit one who is worse off, who supplies to the needy the possession he has as a gift from God and thus becomes a god to his beneficiaries–such a man is an imitator of God."[13]

Beyond explaining the motivations that made them stand out, the *So-Called Letter to Diognetus* details the early Christian's uniqueness. What's remarkable is that these believers not only spoke the words of Jesus with clarity but also lived them with such purity and devotion. You must remember that the Bible, as we know it now, had not been assembled yet. That wouldn't be provided to the church as a complete canon until late in the fourth century. And yet, look at how The So-Called Letter to Diognetus describes Christians.

> They live in their own countries, but only as aliens. They have a share in everything as citizens, and endure everything as foreigners. Every foreign land is their fatherland, and yet for them every fatherland is a foreign land. They marry, like everyone else, and they beget children, but they do not cast out their offspring. They share their board with each other, but not their marriage bed. It is true that they are "in the flesh," but they do not live "according to the flesh." They busy themselves on earth, but their citizenship is in heaven. They obey established laws, but in their own lives they go far beyond what the laws require. They love all men, and by all men are persecuted. They are unknown, and still they are condemned; they are put to death, and yet they are brought to life. They are poor, and yet they make many rich: they are completely destitute, and yet they enjoy complete abundance. They are dishonored, and in their very dishonor are glorified: they are defamed, and are vindicated. They are reviled, and yet they bless; when they are affronted, they still pay due respect. When they do good, they are punished as evildoers; undergoing punishment, they rejoice because they are brought to life. They are treated by the Jews as foreigners and enemies, and are hunted down by the Greeks; and all the time those who hate them find it impossible to justify their enmity.[14]

It's remarkable, isn't it? Convicting too. The early Christians didn't just respond to persecution and their oppressors with love and generosity; they treated everyone and every situation with the same focus and tenacity.

THE CYPRIAN PLAGUE

In 249, the Plague of Cyprian erupted in Ethiopia around Easter. It reached Rome the following year, eventually spreading to Greece and further east to Syria. The plague lasted nearly 20 years and, at its height, reportedly killed as many as 5,000 people per day in Rome.[15] Historians estimate it was responsible for the deaths of up to a fifth of the Roman empire.

Dionysius (AD 200-264), bishop of Alexandria, wrote in a message, "Out of the blue came this disease, a thing more terrifying …than any terror, more frightful than any disaster whatever."[16]

Pontius, Bishop Cyprian's biographer, said, "All were shuddering, fleeing, shunning the contagion, impiously exposing their own friends, as if with the exclusion of the person who was sure to die of the plague, one could exclude death itself also. Meanwhile, there lay about the whole city, no longer bodies, but the carcasses of many, and, by the contemplation of a lot which in their turn would be theirs, demanded the pity of passers-by for themselves. No one regarded anything besides his cruel gains."[17]

Cyprian (AD 210-258), bishop of Carthage, asked his congregation to care for everyone, proclaiming "that there was nothing wonderful in our cherishing only our people with the needed attentions of love, but that one would only become perfect by doing something more than the publican or the heathen, overcoming evil with good, and practicing clemency which was like the divine clemency, loving even his enemies."[18]

Dionysius, bishop of Alexandria, wrote of the church's response to the plague and willingness to sacrifice.

> Our brethren, for the most part, were careless of themselves and with exceeding love and filial kindness clung to one another, visiting the sick without regard to the danger, diligently ministering to them, tending to them in Christ;

> being infected with the disease from others, they drew upon themselves the sickness of their neighbors, willingly taking over their pains. In this manner the best, at any rate, of our brethren departed this life, including certain presbyters and deacons, and same of the laity.[19]

Dionysius claimed, "The heathens behaved in the very opposite way. At the first onset of the disease, they pushed the sufferers away and fled from their dearest, throwing them into the roads before they were dead and treating unburied corpses as dirt."[20]

Christians were different. They regularly practiced caring for the sick, the poor, and the oppressed. Despite the hatred and persecution thrown at them, they did not waver. Regardless of the personal cost to themselves, they were relentless in doing the "work of the ministry," which meant more to them than just preaching the message of Jesus and putting on a weekly service.

In the year 251, Cornelius of Rome wrote a letter to Fabius, bishop of Antioch, in which he listed the leadership structure of the church there: "There are one bishop (for the region in the city), forty-six presbyters, seven deacons, seven subdeacons, forty-two acolytes, first-two exorcists, readers, and doorkeepers." What were these leaders responsible for? Was it the care of a temple, or the spreading of the message? Their exact responsibilities are unclear, however, Cornelius justified this staff by stating that they were responsible for caring for some "1500 widows and distressed persons, all of whom are supported by the grace and loving-kindness of the Master" receiving the church's services in some official way.[21]

THE FOURTH CENTURY

On October 28, 312, Flavius Valerius Constantinus, also known as Constantine the Great, won a great victory over Maxentius at Milvian Bridge, just five kilometers north of Rome. It might have gone down as just another battle for power in Roman history, except that Constantine announced publicly that he had won the battle with the assistance of Jesus Christ. Never before had a Roman emperor confessed he was Christian. On June 13, 313, in partnership with his eastern counterpart, Emperor Licinius, he prepared what is now known as the Edict of Milan. For the first time in the church's history, it was illegal to persecute Christians, and they were under imperial protection. It changed everything. Some believe for the worse. But we will get to that in the next chapter.

In the struggle for the throne after the death of Constantine in 337, Constantius II emerged as emperor, but not before he had massacred many of his own family members to secure power. He followed Constantine's footsteps, maintaining the legalization of Christianity and claimed to be a Christian himself. Upon the death of Constantius in 361, Flavius Claudius Julianus (AD 332-363), also known as Julian "the Apostate" became emperor of Rome.

JULIAN THE APOSTATE

Julian was the nephew of Constantine. Constantius had murdered his father and the majority of his family, and that was something he could not forgive. Because Constantius claimed to be a Christian, Julian hated Christianity to such a degree that he was nicknamed the Apostate. His main goal and passion were to return Rome to its traditional worship of the gods and completely rid the empire of Christianity. He may have succeeded had he not died early, only 18 months into his reign.

He despised Christians, yet he wrote this about them: "Why, then, do we think that this is enough, why do we not observe that it is their benevolence to strangers, their care for the graves of the dead and the pretended holiness of their lives that have done most to increase atheism?" Julian often called Christians atheists because they did not worship the Roman gods. He continued, "I believe that we ought really and truly to practice every one of these virtues. For it is disgraceful that, when no Jew ever has to beg, and the impious Galileans support not only their own poor but ours as well, all men see that our people lack aid from us."[22]

Even in his hatred and disgust, one cannot help but notice his admiration for the Christian's care for the needy. He goes so far as to state that the reason Christianity has been so successful, so irresistible through the ages, was its benevolence and care for the downcast. He laments that because of their care for people, they have more influence than he does.

> We must pay special attention to this point, and by this means effect a cure. For when it came about that the poor were neglected and overlooked by the (pagan temple) priests, then I think the impious Galileans (another term he used for Christians) observed this fact and devoted themselves to philanthropy. And they have gained ascendancy in the worst of their deeds through the credit they win for such practices... The Galileans also begin with their so-called love-feast (open meals), or hospitality, or service of tables–for they have many ways of carrying it out and hence call it by many names–and the result is that they have led very many into atheism.[23]

In another instance, Julian was recorded criticizing the Senate for allowing their wives to sponsor Christianity's efforts to feed the poor: "Every one of you allows his wife to carry everything out of his house to the Galileans, and when your wives feed the poor at your expense they inspire a great admiration for godlessness (Christianity) in those who are in need of such bounty."[24]

OBSERVATIONS OF THE EARLY CHURCH

I'll conclude this walk-through history with a few simple

observations. In the first four centuries, Christianity was known for its actions, not its teaching. It was known for what it stood for and who it stood for, more than it was known for what it stood against. It was recognized, not for what occurred in its weekly gatherings, but for what it did in the cities the other 167 hours of the week. It persevered with its mission to "love" everyone as Jesus loved them, regardless of the opposition. It was so successful in doing these things that the most powerful man in the world at the end of the fourth century lamented for not having the influence the church did.

These observations make me wonder when this all changed. And why did it change? And is it possible to get that influence back?

CHAPTER FOUR

CONSTANTINE CHANGED EVERYTHING

There is no question that Constantine the Great quantifiably changed the landscape of the church. But was his impact positive or negative? That is still up for debate.

Many, including myself, have said this is when everything went wrong in Christian history. I have argued that Constantine legalized the church so that he could monetize and control it. We don't know his motives. Constantine was a complicated man. He may have been seeking to control a movement that had grown to over 10% of the population by the time of his rule, or he could have had a genuine conversion and was seeking to make Jesus known throughout his kingdom. We will never know.

We know that the impact of his decisions and decrees has rippled throughout the centuries, both positively and negatively. You are probably most familiar with the negative ones.

Constantine was the first emperor in history to put a cross on the shields and helmets of his warriors. The church, once bullied, would become bullies themselves. Over 700 years later, kings used this same cross as a banner and rallying cry to launch the Great Crusades. Christians, once dominated, sought to dominate the whole world with force instead of love. Christendom displaced Christianity.

Most of the arguments against Constantine point out that once Christianity became the state religion, it used this power to dominate the masses. The church, once powerless, became egregiously powerful, wealthy, and violent. Roman historians are slightly more cautious about crediting Constantine with this turning point in church history. In all fairness, these gross violations of the heart of Jesus and the mission of the church did not happen in excess until far after he died. As we learned in the previous chapter, Constantine's nephew, Julian the Apostate, sought to overturn everything he had set into place. Under his rule, Christians were once again despised and hunted.

THE EDICT OF MILAN

The truth is Constantine did not make Christianity the state religion. He and his counterpart, Licinius, legalized the freedom of worship in the Edict of Milan. It read:

> Freedom and full liberty has been granted in accordance with the peace of our times, to exercise free choice in worshiping as each one has seen fit. This has been done by us so that nothing may seem to be taken away from anyone's honor or from any religion whatsoever.

This statement doesn't seem abnormal to us who live in a democracy today, but it was the first of its kind. It would have shaken the empire. Constantine and Licinius gave reasons for this surprising Edict. They said, "We believed that we should give both to Christians and to all men the freedom to follow religion, whichever one each one chose," continuing they said, "so that whatever sort of Divinity there is in heavenly regions may be gracious and propitious to us and to all who live under our government."[1]

While freedom of worship was granted with the Edict of Milan, Christianity wouldn't become the official state religion of Rome until 380 under Emperor Theodosius I. Constantine died in 337.

Scholars have debated back and forth over the last 1700 years about Constantine and his impact on Christianity. I am sure there will be many more debates. History is a complicated thing. It is a crazy combination of good and evil, love and hate, bullies and saints. We can ignore what we don't like in history, but we can never fully erase it. It happened. We can learn from it—the good and the bad. Constantine contributed good, and he contributed things that were bad. He was human, after all.

Let's look at Constantine's impact on the church for our study's sake. But let's look at it from a different angle this time. In particular, what did the church do during and after Constantine? Did their ministry to the "least of these" change? Or, once they gained seats of power, did they abdicate this responsibility?

CHRISTIANITY DURING CONSTANTINE

Let's begin during the reign of Constantine. Can you imagine being a Christian in that day? It's difficult to convey how strange the turn of events would have felt to the church. One day, they were outlawed, hunted, persecuted, and killed. The next day, they received imperial protection with all of its benefits. To assume that what Constantine did was negative on the church would be to discount the church of his day. It wasn't negative to them. It was freedom. For multitudes of them, it was life. But it must have also been a confusing time. All they knew was being the hunted, despised, and considered the least of society.

I must pause our history lesson and give credit to where credit is due. Regardless of what we will uncover in the church from

Constantine until now, in my opinion, the most impressive time in the history of the church is its first 300 years. Why? Because while they were the lowest of society, they helped the least of these. They helped the oppressed when they were oppressed. They offered pity when they were the most pitiful. They gave hope when their situation was hopeless. They lifted people up when all of society pushed them down. I feel like taking a moment to give them a standing ovation. What an amazing legacy!

Surprisingly, when Constantine changed their societal position, the church didn't stop its mission. I assumed that the church lost its way when Constantine legalized Christianity. But that was not the case. If anything, Constantine made it possible for them to increase their outreach. He made several changes to the laws during his reign that set up the church's benevolence programs for the next 1500 years! Here are a few examples.

THE EXPOSURE LAWS

Exposure was common practice in Rome and Greece in those days. It was the ancient world's version of abortion. It started with Romulus, Rome's founder, who decreed in the 8th century BC that no child could be killed "before" his third year "unless" he was deformed. Even the so-called refined and educated Cicero (106-43 BC) in his On the Laws 3.8 stated: "Deformed infants shall be killed." The "deformity" could be an unwanted child, a sickly child, a deformed child or simply a wrong-sex child.[2]

Then came Seneca (4 BC - 65 AD), the great Roman stoic philosopher, who said, "We destroy monstrous births, and we also drown our children if they are born weakly or unnaturally formed; to separate what is useless from what is sound is an act, not of anger, but of reason."[3]

Aristotle (384-322 BC), the Greek philosopher, advised "As to exposing or rearing the children born, let there be a law that no deformed child shall be reared; but on the ground of a number of children, if the regular customs hinder any of those born being exposed, there must be a limit fixed to the procreation of offspring, and if any people have a child as a result of intercourse in contravention of these regulations, abortion must be practised on it (the child)."[4]

Plutarch (46-119 AD), a Greek philosopher, wrote that in State-controlled Sparta:

> Nor was it in the power of the father to dispose of the child as he saw fit (as was his right in most heathen societies). He was obliged to carry (the newborn) child before certain men at a place called Lesche; these men were some of the elders of the tribe to which the child belonged; their business was to carefully view the infant, and, if they found it stout and well made, they gave order for its rearing and allotted to it one of the nine thousand shares of land above mentioned for its maintenance, but, if they found it puny and ill-shaped, ordered it to be taken to what was called the Apothetae ("depository"), a (large cave) under Mt. Taygetus (in the Peloponnese); as thinking it neither for the good of the child itself, nor for the public interest, that it should be brought up, if it did not, from the very outset, appear to be healthy and vigorous.[5]

In 313, 315, and 322, Constantine tried to remove the exposure law. He ruled that "if any parent should report that he has offspring which on account of poverty he is not able to rear, there shall be no delay in issuing food and clothing."[6] He used churches as the welfare distribution centers for this program.[7] It was common practice in those days for the church to adopt the children left for exposure. That is why Paul the Apostle often used the metaphor of adoption to describe what God provided for us through Jesus in salvation.

Constantine made it legal for the church to assist in the rearing of unwanted children and even provided state monies to do so.

THE TAX LAWS

Perhaps the two most impactful laws that greatly empowered the church to increase its benevolent activities came on July 3, 321 and June 329. In the first law, Constantine ruled that "every person shall have the liberty to leave at his death any property that he wishes to the most holy and venerable council of the catholic church." (catholic here meant the whole church).[8] What seemed like a small, insignificant tax concession became one of the church's most significant sources of income for centuries.

In the second significant law, Constantine ruled that "the wealthy must assume secular obligations (through their taxes and public offices), and the poor must be supported by the wealth of the churches."[9] In other words, Constantine mandated that the wealthy upper-class citizens attend to matters of state, while Christians should continue assisting the poor. He granted the church tax-free status because it was the empire's charity arm. This law is still in place today in most nations.

We must never forget the reason the church and its land are tax-exempt: we are to be the nation's main charity arm.

Today, thousands of charities with no ties to the church are responsible for meeting societal needs. That was not the case in Constantine's day. The church was that arm, and because of this one fact, the church had an incredible influence on society.

Church historian Dr. John Dickson said of Constantine in his book Bullies and Saints,

> When the emperor eventually freed churches from persecution and then exempted them from taxation, he was setting loose the largest charitable movement the world would ever see. It

> is an aspect of Christian behavior that has never disappeared. Even during the most opulent, negligent, and violent periods of church history, redressing poverty remained central to the church's calling in the world. It remains so today, even though much of the West's welfare is now also provided by the state and other secular humanitarian agencies.[10]

Armed with imperial protection and benefaction, the church only increased its ministry to the "least of these." One of the greatest examples of this came just thirty years after the death of Constantine.

ST. BASIL OF CAESAREA

In 368-369, a great drought and subsequent famine hit the area around Caesarea (modern-day Turkey). One of the leaders of the church there, Basil, took it upon himself to personally organize a soup kitchen and distribute food to the poor.[11]

His friend, Gregory of Nazianzus, spoke these words at Basil's funeral.

> He gathered together the victims of the famine with some who were but slightly recovering from it, men and women, infants, old men, every age which was in distress, and obtaining contributions of all sorts of food which can relieve famine, set before them basins of soup and such meat as was found preserved among us, on which the poor live. Then, imitating the ministry of Christ, Who, girded with a towel, did not disdain to wash the disciples' feet, using for this purpose the aid of his own servants, and also of his fellow servants, he attended to the bodies and souls of those who needed it, combining personal respect with the supply of their necessity, and so giving them a double relief.[12]

A year after the great drought began, Basil was consecrated as Caesarea's Bishop (overseer) on June 14, 370, and remained in this position until he died in 379. He made a significant impact in just a few short years as Bishop. Gregory summarized the legacy of Bishop Basil by stating, "the support of the poor, the entertainment of strangers, the care of maidens, legislation written and unwritten for the monastic life."[13]

His support of the poor was no small thing. It wasn't his side project. It was the entirety of his focus. Gregory noted that Basil came by this focus honestly, stating that his parents were devout Christians, and they were partly to credit for his benevolence. "The union of his parents, cemented as it was by a community of virtue … was notable for many reasons, especially for generosity to the poor, for hospitality … for the dedication to God of a portion of their property."[14]

Basil lived his life being charitable towards others, even using the personal wealth inherited from his deceased father to care for the poor. And his impact was enormous. The poor and needy soon flocked to Basil and the church for help to such a degree that it overwhelmed the city of Caesarea. A new community was designed to care for the destitute, a place that grew so large it became its own city.

Gregory of Nazianzus described this phenomenon, "Go forth a little way from the city (Caesarea), and behold the new city, the storehouse of piety, the common treasury of the wealthy, in which the superfluities of their wealth, aye, and even their necessities, are stored, in consequence of his exhortations, freed from the power of the moth, no longer gladdening the eyes of the thief, and escaping both the emulation of envy, and the corruption of time: where disease is regarded in a religious light, and disaster is thought a blessing, and sympathy is put to the test."[15]

The new city was named Basilead in honor of its founder. The city was a healthcare center and included six separate departments: one for the poor, another for the homeless and strangers, a house for orphans and babies (the church was still adopting children abandoned through the remaining exposure practices), a completely isolated section for lepers, rooms for the aged and infirm, and a proper hospital for the sick. In fact, Basil's hospital was the first public hospital in history and was the inspiration for modern hospitals today.

Gary Ferngren, Professor of History at Oregon State University, said of Basil's inspiration, "Hospitals quickly expanded throughout the Eastern Empire in the late fourth and fifth centuries with bishops taking the initiative in founding them."[16]

Gregory of Nazianzus was so inspired by Basil and, in particular, by Basilead that he wrote *Oration 14* to the church called *"On Love for the Poor."* In it, he concluded, "We must regard charity as the first and greatest of the commandments since it is the very sum of the Law and the Prophets," and "its most vital part I find is the love of the poor along with compassion and sympathy for our fellow man. We must, then, open our hearts to all the poor and to all those who are victims of disasters from whatever cause." Gregory went so far as to compare Basilead to the Seven Wonders of the World.[17]

Does the fact that he drew this comparison make Basil a rare phenomenon and, in doing so, discredit what the rest of the church was doing to help the poor? In some ways, it could. It puts an unusual amount of attention on Basil and elevates him above what other Christians did in the same period and beyond. I don't want to take away any credit from Basil. What he did was amazing! However, I want to highlight that he wasn't the only Christian caring for the needy.

OTHER FOURTH CENTURY HEROES

In 390, in Rome, a Christian woman named Fabiola gained

control over much wealth by divorcing her abusive husband. It is said that she sold her vast properties and distributed everything to the poor. According to her friend, Jerome of Bethlehem, part of this wealth went to an "infirmary."

He described it in detail, saying that Fabiola "gathered into it sufferers from the streets, giving a nurse's care to poor bodies worn with sickness and hunger–maimed noses, lost eyes, scorched feet, leprous arms, swollen bellies. How often she carried on her own shoulders poor filthy wretches tortured by epilepsy! How often did she wash away the purulent matter from wounds while others could not even endure to look at! She gave food with her own hand, and even when a man was but a breathing corpse, she would moisten his lips with drops of water."[18]

Basil's sister, Macrina was another excellent example of charity in this period. She was also wealthy, and, like Fabiola, she sold her estate and gave everything to the poor. It is said she lived her years in a community with other contemplative women who studied, prayed and worked a farm to sustain themselves. Together, these women also rescued infants who had been left abandoned. They raised the children within the community.[19]

In 380, a group of apostolic leaders released a collection of 8 books called *The Constitutions of the Holy Apostles*. This document intended to serve as a manual of guidance for the clergy and, to some extent, for the laity.[20] One of the items it mandated was that bishops should pay the most attention to the most vulnerable, "exhibiting to the orphans the care of parents; to the widows the care of husbands; to those of suitable age, marriage; to the artificer, work; to the unable, commiseration; to the strangers, a house; to the hungry, food; to the thirsty, drink; to the naked, clothing; to the sick, visitation; to the prisoners, assistance."[21]

Again, the church focused on caring for the needy and impacting society with love and dignity. But why did the apostolic leaders of the church need to mandate this? Had the focus on the "least of these" waned to the degree that it needed to be mandated in a constitution?

While these questions must be asked, there is no evidence that we are aware of that indicates a slowing of these activities. However, something else significant was happening at the same time that would introduce us to the next monumental figure in church history, Bishop Ambrose of Milan (339-397 AD).

THE DRIFT TOWARD CHRISTENDOM

In the years following Constantine's new legislation that freed Christians everywhere and gave the church financial support from the state, something very predictable began to happen. The upper class and nobility began to accept Christianity and join the church, and not all of them sold everything to serve the poor.

It is important to remember that Constantine made a law in June of 329 that forbade the noble elites from joining the clergy. Only six years after Constantine died, 170 Bishops gathered in 343 for the Council of Serdica. Among the things discussed at this council was whether they should allow the rich to become bishops. Bishop Hosius of Corduba (256-359 AD) spoke up and said:

> This also I think it necessary for you to consider most carefully, that if perchance some rich man or professional advocate or ex-official be desired for bishop, he be not ordained until he has fulfilled the ministry of a reader and the office of deacon and presbyter, and so ascend, if he has shown himself worthy, through the several grades to the height of the episcopate. For by these promotions which in any case take a considerable length of time can be tested his faith, his discretion, his gravity and modesty. And if he be found worthy, let him be honored with the divine sacerdotal office [i.e. the episcopate]. For it is not fitting, nor does order or discipline allow, that one be

> rashly or lightly ordained bishop, presbyter or deacon, who is a novice, especially since also the blessed Apostle, the teacher of the Gentiles, is seen to have expressly forbidden it. But those [should be ordained] whose life has been tested and their merit approved by length of time.[22]

The council immediately agreed and decreed it as a law for the church. Why was this trying period of a bishop so specific to the rich and powerful? It seemed like the leadership of the church was nervous about the potential danger of wealth and power creeping into their ranks.

Their ruling did not last.

Ambrose had come to Milan as imperial governor in 370. He was already a devout Christian, but in 374, when Bishop Auxentius died, Ambrose went to the church where the election for the next bishop was to take place. His address was interrupted by a call, "Ambrose, bishop!" which was taken up by the whole assembly.[23] In an uncommon fashion, he was parachuted straight into the role of bishop, not having held either the position of deacon or priest in the church beforehand.

As bishop, he immediately shifted his lifestyle and, like Fabiola and Macrina, apportioned his money to the poor, donating all of his lands and making only provision for his sister Marcellina. This raised his popularity even further; it was his popularity with the people that gave him considerable political leverage throughout his career.[24]

He used that popularity to even challenge the emperor Theodosius once, banning him from taking communion until he repented for a massacre of seven thousand civilians in Thessalonica. The emperor complied. That may not be shocking in today's world with the power of the pope and bishops. But, this kind of power being flexed from the church on an imperial level was unheard of in his day.

He was incredibly popular, and his intentions seemed noble. Still, Ambrose's ordination as Bishop and his subsequent career in ministry was as significant to the formation of Western Christianity and Christendom as Constantine's Edict of Milan had been 60 years earlier. Maybe more so.

Princeton's Peter Brown said it was the real "turning point in the Christianization of Europe."[25] He went on to say that because of the ordination of Ambrose, "the gap between the Forum and the church, which had seemed considerable a generation before, came to be closed."[26]

Like history tends to be, there is good that came from closing that gap, and there were negative consequences, too. The good that happened was that Christianity dramatically exploded. From the beginning of the 4th Century, when it was the persecuted minority, to the turn of the 5th Century, when it grew into the popular majority, the landscape dramatically shifted. People from every class were becoming believers and comfortably joining the church.

Dr. John Dickson said of the same period, "It is not that elites suddenly took over the church or that the church suddenly became mainly elite. It is rather that the church grew into a unique association."[27] And herein lies the negative impact. The shift didn't happen overnight, but it did happen. The movement was becoming an organization.

CHAPTER FIVE

MOVEMENTS VS. ORGANIZATIONS

> The word "movement" means "to create action," to go from one place to another. Sustaining a movement is about sustaining action. Per Merriam-Webster, the word "organization" means "the act or process of putting the different parts of something in a certain order so that they can be found or used easily." Sustaining an organization is about sustaining order.[1]

Hildy Gottlieb wrote these words in an article published on July 28, 2015, entitled *"Building Movements, Not Organizations."* She was writing for the *Stanford Social Innovation Review: Informing and inspiring leaders of social change,* and although she was primarily writing to business leaders, I couldn't help but put the church under the same microscope.

Did the church go from "creating action" to "sustaining order?" And if so, why? And how?

By the beginning of the fifth century, the movement was

becoming an organization. Please understand that the church up and to this point was not perfect. It had many flaws and many internal battles over theologies and doctrines. But, from what we can tell, they made their main focus "creating action." Namely, their continued ministry to the "least of these" and the "widows and orphans."

Did that stop at the turn of the fourth century? No. Not really. In some ways, the newfound freedom and wealth only increased the ministry to the down and out. What began to shift, however, was the attitude and corporate focus.

When Constantine legalized Christianity, the persecuted became free. The church started to grow exponentially, and with that growth came more wealth and power. Wealth and power are incredible tools, but they are also incredible corruptors. Jesus warned his disciples about this:

> Luke 12:15
> *Then he said to them, "Watch out! Be on your guard against all kinds of greed; life does not consist in an abundance of possessions."*

> Mark 9:35
> *Sitting down, Jesus called the Twelve and said, "Anyone who wants to be first must be the very last, and the servant of all."*

The church's newfound power at the beginning of the fourth century was short-lived and experienced a significant interruption with Emperor Julian in 361-363. He started to persecute the Christians once again. He also set out to attack the church's growing wealth. Julian issued a decree that all titles to lands, rights and immunities bestowed since the reign of Constantine upon the Galileans, as he contemptuously called the Christians, were abrogated and that the money granted to the Church from the revenues of the

State must be repaid.[2]

The church did not take this kindly. When Julian died in battle, only 18 months into his reign, the subsequent successors, beginning with Emperor Jovian, a devout Christian, began reinstating Constantine's legislations. Christians, vowing never again to allow persecution or their rights to be taken, began to move aggressively towards power. Can you blame them? I can't. Yet, decisions made from fear and self-preservation can lead to trouble, no matter how justifiable.

This self-preservation is likely why the church so quickly went back on its law preventing the rich and powerful from becoming bishops, allowing Ambrose to take a prominent position in the church and the nation. The reasoning behind these decisions is understandable, but the impact of these little compromises would ripple from then until now.

A CHANGE IN POSITION

The church, once bullied, would become bullies themselves. The church, once persecuted, would begin to persecute and kill in the name of Christ, and it didn't take long for them to start.

On August 1, 388, incited by their local Bishop, an angry Christian mob burned a Jewish synagogue to the ground in Callinicum, in the Roman province of Osrhoene. Emperor Theodosius ordered the Christians to rebuild the temple. Outraged and angered by the emperor's decree, Bishop Ambrose said that a synagogue is "a home of unbelief, a house of impiety, a receptacle of folly, which God himself has condemned."[3]

When the emperor didn't respond, Ambrose preached against the emperor from his pulpit and refused to give him communion until he rescinded his order. Yes, this was the same incident we covered in the previous chapter, and as we have already learned, the emperor complied. This only emboldened the church, and over the next 35 years, there were multiple reports of acts of violence perpetrated by Christians.

The church received a significant boost on June 16, 391. That's the date that Theodosius I, a Christian Roman emperor, declared Christianity the religion of the empire. He decreed, "No person shall be granted the right to perform sacrifices; no person shall go around the temples; no person shall revere the shrines." Anyone found to have engaged in any of these activities was to be fined "fifteen pounds of gold."[4] Paganism was now illegal, and Christianity was the state religion.

Instead of using this decree as an opportunity to abandon the violence and return to ministering to the poor, the church did the opposite. Emboldened, they began persecuting pagans, outlawing their rituals, and destroying their temples.

Later, in 391, the bishop of Alexandria, Theophilus, ordered the destruction of the Serapeum (a pagan temple) and its conversion into a church. During the destruction, a group of Christian workmen uncovered several cult objects. They gave some of the relics to Theophilus, who had them paraded through the streets so that they could be mocked and ridiculed. The pagans were incensed by this act of desecration and retaliated in a guerrilla-style attack on the Christian population of Alexandria. Many were killed in the battle that ensued, and in the end, the Christians were victorious, vandalizing and demolishing the Serapeum.[5] The church was flexing its muscles. No longer was it too weak to fight back.

THE DEATH OF AN EMPIRE

While the church grew in strength and power at the beginning of the fifth century, Rome collapsed. The combination of a rising church and the death of an empire created an unexpected power shift. Christianity stepped into the void in many ways and birthed the next global superpower, Christendom.

The empire's demise began in earnest on August 24, 410, when the Visigoths, led by their king Alaric, sacked Rome. This was the first time in almost 800 years that Rome had fallen to a foreign enemy, and it shook the entire world. St. Jerome, living in Bethlehem at the time, wrote, "The city which had taken the whole world was itself taken."[6]

Pelagius, a Roman monk from Britain, survived the siege and wrote an account of the experience in a letter to a young woman named Demetrias.

> This dismal calamity is but just over, and you yourself are a witness to how Rome that commanded the world was astonished at the alarm of the Gothic trumpet, when that barbarous and victorious nation stormed her walls, and made her way through the breach. Where were then the privileges of birth, and the distinctions of quality? Were not all ranks and degrees leveled at that time and promiscuously huddled together? Every house was then a scene of misery and equally filled with grief and confusion. The slave and the man of quality were in the same circumstances, and everywhere the terror of death and slaughter was the same, unless we may say the fright made the greatest impression on those who had the greatest interest in living.[7]

You can sense the shock and confusion. Their world was turned upside down. Adding to the confusion, the Visigoth army withdrew from Rome after three days of pillaging and looting. King Alaric would die of illness only a few months after the attack. The destruction, the humiliation, and now the void of leadership left in the city caused the whole world to feel vulnerable and confused.

Meanwhile, the Roman Empire remained in the middle of the religious conflict between pagans and Christians. The sack of the city was used by both sides to bolster their competing claims of divine legitimacy.[8] Adding fuel to the fire for the Christians, King Alaric left the two main Christian Basilicas in Rome untouched while destroying the pagan temples and burning the Senate House. In fact, many pagans took refuge in the churches during the attack.

AUGUSTINE

In response to this event, Augustine wrote his famous work, *The City of God* to console the Christians in Rome. He made a strong argument for the truth of Christianity over competing religions and philosophies, stating that Christianity was not responsible for the Sack of Rome but instead responsible for Rome's success.[9] This piece of literature would become foundational in shaping Christian theology in the West from then until now.

I don't believe Augustine intended *The City of God* to be used as an argument to justify replacing the Roman Empire with Christendom, but in any case, many of his words were used to that end. Toward the conclusion of *The City of God*, Augustine wrote:

> But, say they, the wise man will wage just wars. As if he would not all the rather lament the necessity of just wars, if he remembers that he is a man; for if they were not just he would not wage them, and would therefore be delivered from all wars. For it is the wrongdoing of the opposing party which compels the wise man to wage just wars; and this wrong-doing, even though it gave rise to no war, would still be matter of grief to man because it is man's wrong-doing. Let every one, then, who thinks with pain on all these great evils, so horrible, so ruthless, acknowledge that this is misery. And if any one either endures or thinks of them without mental pain, this is a more miserable plight still, for he thinks himself happy because he has lost human feeling.[10]

These words were the justification the kings of England used centuries later to declare "Holy War " on the Moors to launch the great crusade to expand Christendom. They are also the words Western kings and presidents have used ever since to justify acts of war. Augustine's words gave Christians, at the end of the first millennium, justification to continue committing acts of violence in the name of Christ.

In her Stanford article, Hildy Gottlieb said,

> Movements begin with values. In successful movements, decisions and actions align with those values. Organizations begin with actions, reinforced by axioms. Values are rarely used as the consistent barometer for determining which actions to take.[11]

I can't help but think that the Crusades were an action reinforced with the axiom "holy war" by so-called Christians who had lost sight of the values of their Savior. In particular, they overlooked Jesus' instructions to "love one another as I have loved you," "bless those who persecute you," and "love your enemies."

Augustine's "just wars" were not the only unintended consequence of the over four hundred thousand words he wrote in *The City of God*. Oxford's Henry Chadwick said of Augustine, "He would have been greatly astonished by the medieval canonists who interpreted him to imply that the empire ought to be run by bishops with the pope at their head."[12]

Another indication that the movement was becoming an organization was its shift in purpose. Hildy Gottlieb said:

> Movements define success globally. If a movement is successful, things change for everyone. Organizations, on the other hand, often define success internally, by what the organization

accomplishes for itself.[13]

In the early 400s, the church shifted its attention from reaching the "least of these" to winning its war with the pagans. It seemed more focused on being right and dominating than serving the greater good. This shift wasn't instantaneous and could be seen as understandable given the circumstances, yet it was monumental and must be noted.

Notably, Augustine's mentor was Bishop Ambrose. This might explain why his writings seemed to come from a different position than had been seen by earlier Christian writers. Christians were no longer on the bottom end of the totem pole, and they were rising. Augustine and the circumstances, namely the weakening of the empire, seemed to push them into a full-fledged organization–Christendom.

THE POPE

The church gained more power on June 6, 445, when Emperor Theodosius II and Valentinian III proclaimed the Roman bishop "as Rector of the whole Church."[14] The decree recognized the primacy of the bishop of Rome based on the merits of Saint Peter, the dignity of the city, and the Nicene Creed; ordained that any opposition to his rulings, which were to have the full force of ecclesiastical law, should be treated as treason; and provided for the forcible extradition by provincial governors of anyone who refused to answer a summons to Rome.

The final collapse of the empire happened toward the end of the fifth century. In 473, the barbarian warrior Odacer killed the boy emperor Romulus Augustulus. Many historians believe this to be the official date the Roman Empire ended. Others believe the date to be 493, when a new Gothic leader named Theodoric killed Odoacer, overtook Italy and established a new regime they called "the Roman empire continued."[15]

The barbarian leadership was weak. Those in Rome and the empire looked to the church for leadership and stability. The church now owned significant buildings and estates on the east part of the city, mainly thanks to lands donated to the church 150 years previously by Constantine. The Vatican exists on those lands to this day. Surprisingly, the barbarians didn't resist the church and maintained good relations with its leadership. The bishop of Rome maintained his position and power over the empire and was looked to as a mayor-type leader within the city, thanks to the precedent set by Bishop Ambrose a century before. The citizens, not just in the city itself, began calling the bishop of Rome "papa" or pope.

Christendom was firmly established. It even had its own king now. Emperor Justinian solidified the supreme leadership of the pope even further in the 6th Century. I cannot overstate Justinian's impact on the church and its role in the world.

EMPEROR JUSTINIAN

Shortly after Justinian became emperor in 527, he decided the empire's legal system needed repair. Three codices of imperial laws and other individual laws existed, many of which conflicted or were outdated. So, in February 528, Justinian created a ten-man commission to review these earlier compilations as well as individual laws, eliminate everything unnecessary or obsolete, make changes as they saw fit, and create a single compilation of imperial laws in force.[16]

The commission finished its work in fourteen months, and the compilation was promulgated in April 529. However, this compilation did not eliminate all of the conflicts over the years in Roman jurisprudence, and the constitutions in the Code were to be used alongside the conflicting opinions of ancient jurists. Justinian attempted to harmonize these conflicting opinions by issuing his

"Fifty Decisions" and by passing additional new laws. Thus, Justinian ordered a new compilation to supersede the first, and this Codex was published in 534. Known as the Codex Repetitae Praelectionis, this second edition of the Code was published on November 16, 534, and took effect on December 30.[17]

The *International Journal of Humanities and Social Science* published a report in January of 2017 stating:

> The year 538 A.D. became the turning point in the history of the Roman Empire since so many aspects on political, administrative and economical levels were already switched off that when Justinian declared himself to be a theologian from this year and no longer a soldier, he crossed the barrier of his mandate between what is purely civil obligation and what is religious obligation, similarly to Constantine before, and entered in competition with the papal function and this role is evidence of Justinian's ongoing caesaropapism. The quest for unification of the empire by unification of the church, the fever for church-building projects with his wife Theodora, the persecution of enemies of the church and heretics, his disdain with the Sabbath although his second name was Sabbatini, his support for suppressing any eschatological fever in line with the church fathers and Oecumenius and yet trying to build the 'Kingdom of God' on earth, all this indicate the problem 538 was for the Roman Empire and the Catholic Church.[18]

The church had an emperor make an entire Codex of laws to establish its "Kingdom of God on earth"-Christendom. The *International Journal of Humanities and Social Science* report, which included professors worldwide, said, "The code of Justinian became a handy tool in the hands of the successors in ecclesiastical circles in Middle-Age legal systems. This biased legal system led to the persecution of many people during the period between 538 and 1798. When the new Catholic Canon Law came out, the role of Justinian in its design was fully recognized. Justinian was the great compiler of a legal system that brought together ecclesiastical related matters to the civil law from the time of Constantine to his own and presented his world in 534 A.D. with a code mixed with Christian religion and state matters. He recognized only one religion, and that is the Christian Orthodox religion with the supreme head at Rome."[19]

I bring this up not to create a debate on the separation of church and state but only to bring to our attention that the status of the church worldwide had significantly shifted by the 6th Century, and with that shift, a new attitude was forming. Jesus' mandate to "go into all the world and preach the gospel" became state-driven instead of an individual responsibility. Instead of a movement of love, it became an organization of power and control. The state law required the church to have a supreme head in Rome. This was interesting because Emperor Justinian was the Byzantine emperor (the eastern part of the empire). He wasn't even ruling from Rome.

THE HOLY ROMAN EMPIRE

These laws set up the next major power move of the church. In 768, Charlemagne became King of the Franks and began an extensive expansion of the realm. He eventually incorporated the territories of present-day France, Germany, northern Italy, the Low Countries and beyond. In 797, the Eastern Roman Emperor Constantine VI was removed from the throne by his mother Irene, who declared herself Empress. As the Latin Church only regarded a male Roman Emperor as the head of Christendom, Pope Leo III sought a new candidate. Charlemagne's exemplary service to the Church in his defense of Papal possessions against the Lombards made him the ideal candidate. On Christmas Day of 800, Pope Leo III crowned Charlemagne emperor, restoring the title in the West for the first time in over three centuries. Charlemagne adopted the formula *Renovatio imperii Romanorum* ("renewal of the Roman Empire"), and so birthed the "Holy Roman Empire." It's impossible to miss the church's role and the Pope's power in these times. The Popes were now king-makers.[20]

In 962, Otto was crowned emperor by Pope John XII, thus intertwining the affairs of the German kingdom with those of Italy and the Papacy. Otto's coronation as Emperor marked the German kings as successors to the Empire of Charlemagne, which also made them consider themselves successors to Ancient Rome.[21]

Otto was known for creating the imperial church system, known as the "Ottonian Church System of the Reich."[22] The imperial church system was a governance policy that entrusted the secular government of the state to as many celibate members of the clergy (especially bishops and abbots) of the Catholic Church as possible instead of the non-celibate laity. Otto did this because celibate clergymen could not produce legitimate heirs who could claim their inheritance at death, thus not establishing regional dynasties that could threaten the ruling family's power. Upon their deaths, the areas governed by celibate clerics automatically reverted to the ruler, who could then appoint their new confidants to the position and thus retain control of all parts of the realm. The system worked as long as the emperors and kings could control the appointment of the bishops. The Ottonians even managed to control the bishops of Rome.[23]

And so began a time of great tension between kings and priests. The Ottonian system worked until the eleventh and twelfth centuries when the popes managed to strengthen their position and called on the bishops to openly oppose the emperor.[24]

In 1049, Pope Leo IX called the Council of Reims, where they adopted a dogmatic declaration about the primacy of the Roman Pontiff, stating: "It was declared that only the bishop/pontiff of the see of Rome is the primate of the universal Church and apostolic"). The bishop of Rome became the official Pope of the entire empire with "full, supreme, and universal power over the whole Church, a power which he can always exercise unhindered, a power that it attributes also to the entire body of the bishops united with the pope. The power that it attributes to the pope's primatial authority has limitations that are official, legal, dogmatic, and practical."[25]

And, so, the church gave itself unhindered power. This emboldened the next move.

THE WAR BETWEEN CHURCH AND STATE

In 1077, the reform-minded Pope Gregory VII was determined to oppose the Ottoniah system and challenged Henry IV (1056–1106 AD), the King of the Romans and Holy Roman Emperor. Henry IV fought back and persuaded his bishops to excommunicate the Pope, whom he famously addressed by his born name, "Hildebrand," rather than his regnal name, "Pope Gregory VII." The Pope, in turn, excommunicated the king, declared him deposed, and dissolved the oaths of loyalty made to Henry. The king found himself with almost no political support and was forced to make the infamous *Walk to Canossa* in 1077.[26] By doing so, he lifted the excommunication at the price of humiliation.

Meanwhile, the German princes had elected another king, Rudolf of Swabia. Henry managed to defeat Rudolf but was subsequently confronted with more uprisings, renewed excommunication, and even the rebellion of his sons. After his death, his second son, Henry V, reached an agreement with the pope and the bishops in the 1122 *Concordat of Worms,* which gave the church complete control over its choice of pope and bishops without interference. The political power of the empire was maintained. Still, the conflict had demonstrated the limits of the ruler's power, especially regarding the church, and it robbed the kings of the sacral status they had previously enjoyed. The pope had surfaced as a significant player in all aspects of the empire, including politically.[27]

There were many other power struggles between the thirteenth and sixteenth centuries, including a significant conflict within the church between several papal claimants, two anti-popes and the "legitimate" Pope. The conflict ended only with the Council of Constance in 1414–1418. Its effect was devastating to the church. The medieval idea of unifying all Christendom into a single political entity, with the Church and the Empire as its leading institutions, began to decline.[28]

The combination of this decline, the obvious corruption, and abuses of power led to the most significant major division in the church and empire following the Protestant Reformation led by Martin Luther in 1517. The empire was divided along religious lines, with the north, the east, and many of the major cities, including Strasbourg, Frankfurt, and Nuremberg, becoming Protestant, while the southern and western regions remained predominantly Catholic.

THE CHURCH DIVIDED

The Reformation was necessary. The church had long been corrupt, greedy and power-hungry. It desperately needed to be reformed. But it would be incredibly naive to think that the Reformation repaired all that. The Protestant Church may have removed the primacy of an empirical bishop of the church, but it still tried to control nations and kings. It may have been marching under a different banner, but it was still trying to build Christendom, an earthly kingdom of religion.

The idea of building an earthly kingdom in the name of God has been a problem since the time of Jesus. The God-fearing Jews missed Jesus as their promised Messiah because they were wanting and expecting the Messiah to establish an earthly, Jewish-dominated kingdom. But Jesus said, *"My kingdom is not of this world. If it were, my servants would fight to prevent my arrest by the Jewish leaders. But now my kingdom is from another place."*[29]

We lose our purpose as a church when we try building Christendom, a dominating earthly kingdom, instead of building the Kingdom of God. We also lose our identity when we get these kingdoms confused. I don't know about you, but I am convicted by how easy it is to confuse the two. I do it all of the time.

The lines are often so blurred that finding the path forward is hard. But remember, when you get lost, the best way to find your way again is to go back, retrace your steps, and find the place where you were on the right track. That's why I wanted you to become familiar with church history. We need to be familiar with when the church got it right and when it didn't so that we can find our way back to the bullseye again.

CHRISTENDOM VS. CHRISTIANITY

Can you see it now? Do you understand the stark differences between Christendom and Christianity? Are you recognizing when we're off the mark?

According to Stuart Murray in his book Post-Christendom, the Christendom shift meant:

- The adoption of Christianity as the official civil religion of a city, state, or empire;
- The movement of the church from the margins of society to its center;
- The creation and progressive development of a Christian culture or civilization;
- The assumption that all citizens (except for Jews) were Christian by birth;
- The development of the corpus Christianum, where there was no freedom of religion and where political power was

regarded as divinely authenticated;

- Infant baptism as the symbol of obligatory incorporation into this Christian society;
- Sunday as an official day of rest and obligatory church attendance, with penalties for noncompliance;
- The definition of "orthodoxy" as the common belief shared by all, which was determined by powerful church leaders supported by the state;
- The imposition of a supposedly Christian morality on the entire society (although normally Old Testament moral standards were applied);
- A hierarchical ecclesiastical system based on a diocesan and parish arrangement, which was analogous to the state hierarchy and was bolstered by state support;
- The construction of massive and ornate church buildings and the formation of huge congregations;
- A generic distinction between clergy and laity and the relegation of the laity to a largely passive role;
- The increased wealth of the church and the imposition of obligatory tithes to fund this system;
- The defense of Christianity by legal sanctions to restrain heresy, immorality, and schism;
- The division of the globe into "Christendom" or "heathendom" and the waging of war in the name of Christ and the church;
- The use of political and military force to impose the Christian faith; and
- The use of the Old Testament, rather than the New, to support and justify many of these changes.[30]

Ouch! Did you notice all of the wrong notes being played in the list above? We are still playing many of these melodies distinctly different from the one Jesus designed.

Why does every American President feel the need to declare that they are a Christian? Why do they feel the need to name their pastor? Remember President Trump posing with a Bible in front of St. John Episcopal Church? Christendom or Christianity? Don't blame him. We have empowered this behavior.

Canadians, we're not off the hook either. Why do Canadian pastors feel empowered to stand up to the government to demand their right to gather weekly, shoulder to shoulder, in a temple?

The church has been trying to control politics and politicians for centuries. That's not our job. Jesus didn't tell us to do that. He didn't tell us to defend ourselves or our rights. He didn't ask us to build castles. He asked us to expand His Kingdom. He instructed us to be a movement "committed to action."

Jesus said to go preach the gospel to all men, period. He said to love as he loved. He said to feed the hungry, give water to the thirsty, clothe the naked, shelter the homeless, visit those in prison, and minister to the sick. That's Kingdom-building. It doesn't feed our craving for power, but it empowers us. And it does create influence.

Matthew 23:1-12
Then Jesus said to the crowds and to his disciples: "The teachers of the law and the Pharisees sit in Moses' seat. So you must be careful to do everything they tell you. But do not do what they do, for they do not practice what they preach. They tie up heavy, cumbersome loads and put them on other people's shoulders, but they themselves are not willing to lift a finger to move them. "Everything they do is done for people to see: They make their phylacteries wide and the tassels on their garments long; they love the place of honor at banquets and the most important seats in the synagogues; they love to be greeted with respect in the marketplaces and to be called 'Rabbi' by others. "But you are

> *not to be called 'Rabbi,' for you have one Teacher, and you are all brothers. And do not call anyone on earth 'father,' for you have one Father, and he is in heaven. Nor are you to be called instructors, for you have one Instructor, the Messiah. The greatest among you will be your servant. For those who exalt themselves will be humbled, and those who humble themselves will be exalted.*

Jesus promised greatness, but not by demanding it or taking it by force. Greatness in the Kingdom of God comes from serving. The church of the first three centuries proved this to be true. They served to the degree that they gained influence and power. Once they had that power, they feared losing it, and their focus shifted to self-protectionism, and the movement became an organization, something Jesus never intended it to be. We need to rediscover our purpose.

Where do we start?

Nehemiah noticed the state of his city, wept for days, accepted personal and corporate responsibility and repented. When I learn of our history as a church and analyze our current state, I am moved to tears, too. God help us! I hope you feel the same way. But that feeling isn't enough. We must do something about it. Pointing the finger at the past leaders or looking for modern pastors and leaders to blame is not the answer. Where we cast blame is where we assign responsibility, and whoever is assigned responsibility is given the ability to respond. We must accept personal and corporate responsibility for where we have missed the target.

The second thing Nehemiah did was re-anchor himself in his identity. It is too easy to confuse which kingdom we are building when we don't understand our Kingdom identity. Let's rediscover together our God-given Kingdom identity. That's what we will attempt to do in the next section of this book.

SECTION TWO

KNOW YOUR IDENTITY

CHAPTER SIX

JESUS IS KING

Who am I that I can repent and accept responsibility for the church? What difference could I make?

Nehemiah must have had similar thoughts when he heard the report on the state of his city. He could have easily made excuses as to why he wasn't the one who should rebuild Jerusalem. He was a prisoner of war, kept against his will, with no freedom to go where he wanted when he wanted. He was also currently positioned as a cupbearer for the king himself. What would he know about rebuilding a city? Because he was a direct servant to the king, there would be no way the king would allow him to leave, especially to rebuild Jerusalem. Besides, rebuilding a city would take an army of men and women. Who would follow a lowly servant, prisoner of war, or cupbearer?

I don't know if Nehemiah had these thoughts, but I would've doubted myself in the same situation. I make excuses in circumstances far less cumbersome than the one Nehemiah was in. Excuses are our kryptonite. They strip us of our ability to change.

Nehemiah didn't make any excuses. Not one. At least not out loud.

After hearing the report from Jerusalem, Nehemiah went to God in prayer. In the middle of this prayer, he said these words, "*They are Your servants and Your people whom You redeemed by Your great power and by Your strong hand.*"[1]

At first glance, this prayer looks like Nehemiah justifying to God, and primarily to himself, the reason the Israelites deserved to be rescued. But, I also believe that in the process of reminding God who the Israelites were to Him, he reminded himself who he was, too. He was a Jew. That meant that he was part of God's chosen people. He may have been a literal servant to a king, but he was really the servant of the King of kings. His king had the power to kill and destroy but his King had the power to create life and restore it.

Nehemiah had already accepted responsibility, which gave him the ability to respond. Now, he was recentering himself in his true identity, which I believe gave him the courage to respond.

When we look at the history of the church, we can see how far the church has drifted from God's original design. It's easy to blame the past to justify why the melody the church plays today is so far gone from the original score Jesus composed.

For some of you, your personal experience with the church has led you to believe that the original tune is too far gone. It might not even be possible to find it again.

For others, you feel like the tune you have heard and have played is precisely the tune Jesus composed, and you pity those who haven't experienced the church as you have. But what can you do about the rest of the church? You are sad. You are angry with the abuses and gross misrepresentations of the Gospel. You even timidly apologize for the church to anyone who might care to listen. That's good. But what if I told you there is something more you could do? What if you and I could affect more than just our little corners of the world? What if we could become like Nehemiah, Bishop Basil, or Martin

Luther? What if it is true that you and I were made on purpose, for a purpose, for such a time as this?

I wrote this book because I had gotten swallowed up in frustration and then made the subsequent excuses as to why I could not make a significant difference. The ruins I saw were just too overwhelming. Then something awakened in me, and I just have to share it because I believe it will awaken you, too.

To this point of our journey, I have been giving you the report of the state of the church, not to discourage you, and certainly not to tell you something you didn't already know or feel, but to have us come face-to-face with reality as it is.

Let's work our way forward, eliminating the excuses so that you and I can make a significant difference in the future church. It begins where it began with Nehemiah–knowing who we really are. This identity must be anchored in who God says we are, not who we think we are or who the world thinks we are.

I believe this Biblical identity is rooted in Kingdomology, which is the clear understanding of the Kingdom of God. We are not Christian (Christ-like) until we are Kingdom-minded. Jesus didn't come to start a religion. He came to restore a Kingdom.

THE FOUR INGREDIENTS OF A KINGDOM

Let's start with the basics. A kingdom, any kingdom, is comprised of four main things:

1. A King.
   You can't have a kingdom without a king.

2. A territory.
   A king without a territory is not much of a king. Kingdom simply means the domain of a king. Without a domain, you can't be a king.

3. A government.
   The government is simply the laws that govern the kingdom.

4. A people.
   A king must have people to rule, or he is not much of a king.

It's interesting to note that Nehemiah's prayer in Nehemiah 1 was a Kingdom prayer. Knowingly or unknowingly, he revealed all four of these attributes of a kingdom in this short prayer. It might be why God chose to use him to rebuild the city.

Let's look at Nehemiah's prayer again.

> Nehemiah 1:5-11 (NASB)
> *"Please, Lord God of heaven, the great and awesome God, who keeps the covenant and faithfulness for those who love Him and keep His commandments: let Your ear now be attentive and Your eyes open, to hear the prayer of Your servant which I am praying before You now, day and night, on behalf of the sons of Israel Your servants, confessing the sins of the sons of Israel which we have committed against You; I and my father's house have sinned. We have acted very corruptly against You and have not kept the commandments, nor the statutes, nor the ordinances which You commanded Your servant Moses. Remember, please, the word which You commanded Your servant Moses, saying, 'If you are unfaithful, I will scatter you among the peoples; but if you return to Me and keep My commandments and do them, though those of you who have been scattered were in the most remote part of the heavens, I will gather them from there and bring them to the place where I have chosen to have My name dwell.' They are Your servants and Your people whom You redeemed by Your great power and by Your strong hand. Please, Lord, may Your ear be attentive to the prayer of Your servant and the prayer of Your*

servants who delight to revere Your name, and please make Your servant successful today and grant him mercy before this man."

Did you see it?

1. ***"Lord God of heaven, the great and awesome God."***
   Nehemiah hailed God as the highest King. The King of kings. A King higher than the king he served.

2. ***"I will gather them from there and bring them to the place where I have chosen to have My name dwell."***
   Nehemiah listed a territory. Every king must have a territory. And subtly, did you notice it is a territory chosen by Him, not for Him? Again, Nehemiah hailed God as the Supreme ruler. We don't get to decide where He dwells. He does.

3. ***"But if you return to Me and keep My commandments and do them."***
   Nehemiah acknowledged God's laws and government as Moses gave them.

4. ***"They are Your servants and Your people"***
   Nehemiah identifies that the King has a people and, in doing so, also acknowledges that he is a servant of a higher King than the king he could physically serve.

Jesus emphatically instructed His followers to *"seek first the Kingdom of God"* and then the promised result, *"and all these things shall be added to you."*[2] I can't help but think that Nehemiah did just that; he sought the Kingdom of God first, above his circumstances, above his comfort, and his king and God delivered on the promise. He provided "all the things" Nehemiah needed to get the job done.

WHICH KINGDOM ARE WE BUILDING?

The church of the past and the present begins to miss the mark the moment it forgets which Kingdom it is building. The moment we start building our own kingdoms, we are wrong. The moment we confuse Christendom with the Kingdom, we are wrong. The moment we start building and preserving castles instead of the Kingdom, we are wrong. Jesus said, *"seek first..."* That means it's not wrong to build castles or to expand our churches on earth. But it does mean that we are to remember who is King and whose Kingdom is first.

Today's Christians, myself included, can limit Jesus to just a Saviour, a friend, a good teacher, or a prophet. He is all those things, but He is first and foremost a King. Jesus is King. Paul proclaimed it long before Kanye West did. He said in 1 Timothy 1:16-17, *"But for that very reason I was shown mercy so that in me, the worst of sinners, Christ Jesus might display his immense patience as an example for those who would believe in him and receive eternal life. Now to the King eternal, immortal, invisible, the only God, be honor and glory forever and ever. Amen."*

Jesus came preaching the Kingdom. It was reported that He began His ministry and continued it with the purpose of the Kingdom. Matthew said, *"Jesus went throughout Galilee, teaching in their synagogues, proclaiming the good news of the kingdom, and healing every disease and sickness among the people."*[3]

The Kingdom is good news! It's not command and control, oppression and domination. It is good news to all who hear its original melody. When Jesus played it, it was beautiful. When we play it right, it is beautiful too. It is good news.

THE DISCIPLES FINALLY UNDERSTAND THE KINGDOM

Jesus came to re-establish the Kingdom. His disciples didn't understand this at first, but when they got it, they changed the world with this message. In fact, it became their sole focus. The word 'kingdom' appears 167 times in the New Testament.

Look at how close they came to missing it and how easy it is for us to miss it, too:

Luke 24:13-19
Now that same day two of them were going to a village called Emmaus, about seven miles from Jerusalem. They were talking with each other about everything that had happened. As they talked and discussed these things with each other, Jesus himself came up and walked along with them; but they were kept from recognizing him. He asked them, "What are you discussing together as you walk along?" They stood still, their faces downcast. One of them, named Cleopas, asked him, "Are you the only one visiting Jerusalem who does not know the things that have happened there in these days?" "What things?" he asked. "About Jesus of Nazareth," they replied. "He was a prophet, powerful in word and deed before God and all the people."

These are two of His disciples, at the end of His ministry on earth, after the crucifixion, on the day of His resurrection. They had witnessed Jesus heal the sick, raise the dead, walk on water, calm storms with his words, feed the five thousand, and more. Yet in their minds, He was just "a prophet, powerful in word and deed." All of that was about to change for them.

Luke 24:28-34
As they approached the village to which they were going, Jesus continued on as if he were going farther. But they urged him strongly, "Stay with us, for it is nearly evening; the day is almost over." So he went in to stay with them. When he was at the table with them, he took bread, gave thanks, broke it and began to give

it to them. Then their eyes were opened and they recognized him, and he disappeared from their sight. They asked each other, "Were not our hearts burning within us while he talked with us on the road and opened the Scriptures to us?" They got up and returned at once to Jerusalem. There they found the Eleven and those with them, assembled together and saying, "It is true! The Lord has risen and has appeared to Simon."

Before they recognized who Jesus really was, they worshiped Him as Savior, a prophet who did miracles and taught well, but afterwards, they saw Him as King. They proclaimed, "The Lord has risen." Lord is a big word in this sentence. Lord denotes more authority than Savior, prophet or miracle worker. Lord means "owner" and King.

Still, Thomas, one of the twelve, didn't believe their report.

John 20:24-25
Now Thomas (also known as Didymus), one of the Twelve, was not with the disciples when Jesus came. So the other disciples told him, "We have seen the Lord!" But he said to them, "Unless I see the nail marks in his hands and put my finger where the nails were, and put my hand into his side, I will not believe."

It's not that he didn't believe in Jesus or that Jesus was Savior or even Messiah. He just didn't believe Jesus was King.

John 20:26-29
A week later his disciples were in the house again, and Thomas was with them. Though the doors were locked, Jesus came and stood among them and said, "Peace be with you!" Then he said to Thomas, "Put your finger here; see my hands. Reach out your hand and put it into my side. Stop doubting and believe." Thomas

> *said to him, "My Lord and my God!" Then Jesus told him, "Because you have seen me, you have believed; blessed are those who have not seen and yet have believed."*

Did you see it? Thomas proclaimed the same thing as the two disciples on the road to Emmaus. Jesus went from being his Savior to "My Lord and my God!" I wonder if, in our churches today, we have taught a theology that asks people to simply believe in Jesus as Savior and misses the importance of believing in Jesus as King. He is our Savior. He is our friend. He was a good prophet, teacher, and miracle worker. But He is so much more than that. Jesus is King!

You might be thinking, "Ya, I get that." What does that have to do with taking our job back?

Many people believe in God. Big deal. Many people confess they believe in Jesus. Great. But, for us to really be the church and play the original tune Jesus wrote for the church to play, we must fully understand the Composer. He is not easy to understand. Remember, the disciples physically lived with him for three years. They heard every message He spoke, the ones we have recorded, and many more. They personally witnessed the miracles, healings, signs and wonders. They didn't fully grasp who He was before He appeared to them in person, risen from the dead. Multitudes of other people witnessed many of the same spectacles and completely missed God in their midst. If it was difficult for them to grasp, imagine how much more difficult it is for us.

Oh God, please help us see and fully understand!

ARE WE PLAYING THE TUNE RIGHT?

Let me put into context the complexities of what I just said. Imagine being mentored by the great composer Johann Sebastian Bach. You are allowed to sit with him day and night for three years, personally witnessing how he thought, wrote, and performed.

Imagine being an eyewitness to him writing the Brandenburg Concertos and then, after his death, being asked to perform them in public. Would your performance do the concertos justice? Maybe, but maybe not. In your ears, you hear the nuances of how Bach performed them. His swells, emotion, and passion for the music are unmatched. "No one could play it like him," you think to yourself. Yet, you do your best, and people look to you to interpret what was written because you were there! You should know best.

Now imagine centuries after his death, musicians trying to capture the essence of the music. Is what they interpret correct? All they have is what they have written on paper and how they have heard other musicians interpret the same piece. How would we ever know if anyone had interpreted it in the way Bach himself had intended it to be when he wrote it?

While that example is simplistic in its argument, you get the point. The disciples had the daunting task of interpreting Jesus for the rest of the world. Jesus Himself recognized how difficult it would be for those who had seen Him in the flesh and how daunting it would be for those who had not seen Him. Daunting, yes, but not impossible.

How do we know when we play it right? Jesus told us.

Matthew 7:15-20

Watch out for false prophets. They come to you in sheep's clothing, but inwardly they are ferocious wolves. By their fruit you will recognize them. Do people pick grapes from thornbushes, or figs from thistles? Likewise, every good tree bears good fruit, but a bad tree bears bad fruit. A good tree cannot bear bad fruit, and a bad tree cannot bear good fruit. Every tree that does not bear good fruit is cut down and thrown into the fire. Thus, by their fruit you will recognize them.

Jesus said we would know the right melody from the wrong one by the results. What results was He referring to? Signs and wonders? Not exactly. Remember, the disciples on their way to Emmaus commented on the signs and wonders they saw Jesus perform, yet they still didn't recognize His kingship.

Look at the "fruit" Jesus dismisses in the verses that follow.

Matthew 7:21-23

"Not everyone who says to me, 'Lord, Lord,' will enter the kingdom of heaven, but only the one who does the will of my Father who is in heaven. Many will say to me on that day, 'Lord, Lord, did we not prophesy in your name and in your name drive out demons and in your name perform many miracles?' Then I will tell them plainly, 'I never knew you. Away from me, you evildoers!'

Evildoers? That's a bit harsh, don't you think? Especially when the list of their "evil deeds" includes saying, "Lord, Lord," prophesying in His name, performing miracles, and casting out demons. Yet, Jesus seems unimpressed and even goes so far as to call them evildoers.

So what impresses Him? He tells us in the next verse.

Matthew 7:24- 27

Therefore everyone who hears these words of mine and puts them into practice is like a wise man who built his house on the rock. The rain came down, the streams rose, and the winds blew and beat against that house; yet it did not fall, because it had its foundation on the rock. But everyone who hears these words of mine and does not put them into practice is like a foolish man who built his house on sand. The rain came down, the streams rose, and the winds blew and beat against that house, and it fell with a great crash.

He is impressed when we aren't just hearing and repeating what we heard but doing what He instructs us to do. He is not just looking for talk; He expects action. What kind of action? Prophesying, performing miracles, and casting out devils don't count.

Matthew 25:34
Then the King will say to those on his right, 'Come, you who are blessed by my Father; take your inheritance, the kingdom prepared for you since the creation of the world."

Here is one of those "Kingdom" verses. Jesus is answering a question His disciples asked earlier in Matthew 24. They asked Him, "What will be the sign of your coming and the end of the age?"[4] Jesus answered this question by prophesying in great detail about the coming destruction of Jerusalem, which occurred just as He said it would in 70 A.D. Then, in Matthew 25, He suddenly fast-forwards to prophesying about Judgment Day, the day we all will give an account before the King. Jesus explains what the King is looking for from His servants.

Matthew 25:35-36
For I was hungry and you gave me something to eat, I was thirsty and you gave me something to drink, I was a stranger and you invited me in, I needed clothes and you clothed me, I was sick and you looked after me, I was in prison and you came to visit me.'

Interestingly, the King of kings is less concerned with our paying homage to Him than He is with how we treat others. In particular, He cares about how we treat the "least of these."

Matthew 25:37
"The King will reply, 'Truly I tell you, whatever you did for one of the least of these brothers and sisters of mine, you did for me.'"

How can this be? It seems so backward. Shouldn't the main focus of the subjects in a kingdom be to serve the king? That's how man thinks, but that's not how our King thinks. Our King is not looking for servants. He is looking for sons and daughters, which we'll cover in the next chapter.

OUR KING'S COMMAND

Remember when I quoted Nehemiah's recognition of the "commands" of God as given through Moses? Well, our King, Jesus, gave us commands too. In fact, He gave us just one.

John 13:34-35
"A new command I give you: Love one another. As I have loved you, so you must love one another. By this everyone will know that you are my disciples, if you love one another."

When Jesus said, "A new command I give you," He wasn't adding an additional command to the Ten Commandments and the Old Testament law; He was instituting a replacement command. Jesus intended this command to trump all of the others. He reiterated the same thing in John 15.

John 15:12-17
My command is this: Love each other as I have loved you. Greater love has no one than this: to lay down one's life for one's friends. You are my friends if you do what I command. I no longer call you servants, because a servant does not know his master's business. Instead, I have called you friends, for everything that I learned

> *from my Father I have made known to you. You did not choose me, but I chose you and appointed you so that you might go and bear fruit—fruit that will last—and so that whatever you ask in my name the Father will give you. This is my command: Love each other.*

What a contrast. Jesus said, "You are my friends if you do what I command." Is He our friend, or is He our King? Well, according to Jesus, both! The word 'if' is enormous in this verse. We are His friends 'if' we do His commands to love as He loved.

Easy to say and next to impossible to do.

Love as He loved? Wow! He loved the unlovable, the outcasts, the broken, and the seemingly unredeemable. He died for all of us, and we are supposed to love like that? Impossible.

Jesus knew it would be impossible for humanity. Immediately after He told the disciples His command and expectations as their King, He also told them about the Helper He would send. He said this about the Holy Spirit, *"He will glorify me because it is from me that he will receive what he will make known to you. All that belongs to the Father is mine. That is why I said the Spirit will receive from me what he will make known to you."*[5]

Jesus promised the Holy Spirit would help us live out His command. The purpose of the Holy Spirit is not to give us the power to perform miracles, but instead, He intends to provide us with the power to love as Jesus loved. If that love requires a miracle or a healing, He can help with that, too. It's not about us. It's about Him. It's about our King.

No wonder the Kingdom of God is good news. It's a Kingdom advancing with love, not religion, domination, or control. It's a Kingdom of sons and daughters advancing to serve the "least of these."

JESUS IS KING

Jesus declared His Kingship to Pilate at His trial.

John 18:36-37
Jesus said, "My kingdom is not of this world. If it were, my servants would fight to prevent my arrest by the Jewish leaders. But now my kingdom is from another place." "You are a king, then!" said Pilate. Jesus answered, "You say that I am a king. In fact, the reason I was born and came into the world is to testify to the truth. Everyone on the side of truth listens to me."

In His confession, Jesus stated His purpose: "The reason I was born…" The reason Jesus came to this earth was not to start a religion. He came to re-establish His Kingdom in a territory He had lost.

In the next chapter, we will study that territory because we can easily get lost in our purpose if we don't understand it correctly.

CHAPTER SEVEN

ON EARTH AS IT IS IN HEAVEN

The entire Bible begins with these words, "In the beginning God created the heavens and the earth."[1] Let's break that down for a moment.

"In the beginning *God*." The Bible makes it clear that God was here first.

"In the beginning God *created*." The Bible makes it clear that God is the creator, and because He is the creator, He is the owner. What He creates belongs to Him.

"In the beginning God created the *heavens*." The first thing the Bible lists of God's creation is the heavens. That is important. That means the heavens are His domain.

"In the beginning God created the heavens and the *earth*." The very next thing God created was the earth. The order in which He created is essential, as this sequence reveals His kingdom, including our place in it.

THE KING-DOMAIN

In a kingdom, all the land within the kingdom is the king's personal property, and this ownership designates him as lord. In a kingdom, the territory the king owns is called "crownland." This implies the land is the property of "the crown," referring to the king himself.

I live in Canada, which is still part of the Kingdom of England. That means, at the time of this writing, the land of Canada is solely owned by King Charles III. It is his personal property. Only 9.7% of the total land in Canada is privately owned, while the rest is crownland. The land is administered on behalf of the Crown by various agencies or departments of the government of Canada. The Canadian Act has no provision for any Canadian to own physical land in Canada. Canadians can only own an interest in an estate.[2]

I know. I was surprised, too. But this is because, in a kingdom, all of the land belongs to the king. Every square foot of territory is his personal property—his "king-domain." A king is not a king without a domain. In a true kingdom, therefore, there is no such thing as private property owned by the citizens; the king owns all.[3]

Because God was here first and is the Creator of all things, He is King. God owns the earth and everything in it. It is His crownland. Psalm 24:1 states it plainly: *The earth is the Lord's, and everything in it, the world, and all who live in it.*

Because God is the owner, He can do whatever He pleases with the earth. The Psalmist says He chose to give it to man. It says in Psalm 115:16, *The highest heavens belong to the Lord, but the earth he has given to mankind.*

Genesis 1 clearly describes God giving us the earth to rule on His behalf right at creation.

Genesis 1:26-28

Then God said, "Let us make mankind in our image, in our

> *likeness, so that they may rule over the fish in the sea and the birds in the sky, over the livestock and all the wild animals, and over all the creatures that move along the ground." So God created mankind in his own image, in the image of God he created them; male and female he created them. God blessed them and said to them, "Be fruitful and increase in number; fill the earth and subdue it. Rule over the fish in the sea and the birds in the sky and over every living creature that moves on the ground."*

The first thing God gave man was a territory. He didn't give them a religion. He gave them a garden to rule over. The word "rule" in verse 28 is the Hebrew word mamlakah, which means "kingdom" or "sovereign rule." Don't make the mistake of thinking that because God gave us sovereign rule, we now own it. A king gives land to his subjects to steward, not to own. The king can take back the land and give it to someone else anytime he chooses.

COLONIZATION

This is true in Canada. Canadians aren't given full ownership, and they can "only have an interest in the estate."[4] God made this concept clear to the Israelites through Moses in Leviticus 25.

> Leviticus 25:23-24
> *"'The land must not be sold permanently, because the land is mine and you reside in my land as foreigners and strangers. Throughout the land that you hold as a possession, you must provide for the redemption of the land."*

How did Canada come to be owned by the Kings and Queens of England? They colonized it.

Understanding the concept of colonization is critical to understanding the Kingdom. According to the Webster's Dictionary, a colony is "an area over which a foreign nation or state extends or maintains control" and "a group of people who establish residence in that area and who retain ties with the parent state."[5]

When we understand that God colonized the earth, we gain insight into His original intentions and a deeper understanding of what He is doing now. He created the earth to expand His Kingdom from the supernatural realm to the natural realm. He created mankind to colonize this natural realm. We are citizens of heaven sent to rule the King's territory on earth, influencing it with His culture and values.

Does it seem far-fetched? It shouldn't. The Apostle Paul said, *"But our citizenship is in heaven. And we eagerly await a Savior from there, the Lord Jesus Christ."*[6]

Dr. Myles Monroe said in his book, *Kingdom Principles:*

> The concept of colonization is the most important component of a kingdom that we must understand or else it will be impossible to fully grasp the essence of the message of the Bible, the prophets, and the focus and priority of Jesus Christ. It is the misunderstanding or ignorance of this kingdom concept of colonization that has produced all human religions and sects. Christianity as a religion is itself a product of this misunderstanding. The primary purpose, motive, plan, and program of God the Creator was to colonize earth with Heaven.[7]

When Adam and Eve sinned, they didn't lose a religion. They lost a territory. For a season, the colony changed hands. Jesus came to take it back. He didn't come to start a religion. He came to redeem a territory and firmly re-establish His Kingdom here on earth.

Galatians 4:4-7

But when the set time had fully come, God sent his Son, born of a woman, born under the law, to redeem those under the law, that we might receive adoption to sonship. Because you are his sons, God sent the Spirit of his Son into our hearts, the Spirit who calls out, "Abba, Father." So you are no longer a slave, but God's child; and since you are his child, God has made you also an heir.

In the opening moments of Jesus' public ministry, He proclaimed, *"God's kingdom is here."*[8] He wasn't just announcing that He was back. He was announcing that we were back!

In light of this, He taught His disciples how to pray.

Matthew 6:9-13

"This, then, is how you should pray: "'Our Father in heaven, hallowed be your name, your kingdom come, your will be done, on earth as it is in heaven. Give us today our daily bread. And forgive us our debts, as we also have forgiven our debtors. And lead us not into temptation, but deliver us from the evil one.'"

There is so much in this short prayer that is so revealing to the heart and purposes of Jesus.

THE KING'S LOCATION IS KEY

Jesus taught His disciple to begin prayer by saying, *"Our Father in heaven."* This brief statement not only mentions God's title but also specifies his location. Interesting. Why would mentioning His location be important? Why not just begin with "Our Father" and leave it at that? Jesus did everything on purpose. He wanted His disciples to understand that knowing the location of the King of kings is essential.

A historical example of the importance of a king's location

is the story of the formation of the nation of Brazil. In the early 1800s, Brazil was a colony of Portugal. In an unprecedented move, the Prince Regent (acting king) of Portugal, John VI, anticipated the invasion of Napoleon's army and ordered the transfer of the Portuguese royal court to Brazil before he could be deposed. On January 22, 1808, John VI and his court arrived in Salvador, Brazil.

For thirteen years, Rio de Janeiro, Brazil, functioned as the capital of the Kingdom of Portugal in what some historians call a metropolitan reversal (i.e., a colony exercising governance over the entirety of an empire). The court's time in Rio significantly changed the city and its residents. The move also had profound impacts on Brazilian society, economics, infrastructure, and politics.[9]

Due to the absence of the king and the economic independence of Brazil, Portugal entered a severe political crisis that caused John VI and the royal family to return on April 25, 1821; otherwise, he risked the loss of his Portuguese throne.[10] John VI left his heir, Pedro I, in Brazil to reign in his stead there.

The Portuguese Cortes demanded that Brazil return to its former status as a colony. Prince Pedro, influenced by the Rio de Janeiro Municipal Senate (Senado da Câmara), refused this demand, including the order to return to Portugal. Brazil declared its independence on September 7, 1822, forming the Empire of Brazil and ending 322 years of colonial dominance of Portugal over Brazil.

As you can tell from this historical account, a colony isn't a colony anymore when the king arrives. The arrival of the king changes everything. When Jesus taught his disciples to pray, *"Our Father in heaven,"* He essentially said that the King is on His throne in heaven. God's location is critical to understanding His authority and brings clarity to our authority and responsibilities on earth.

When Jesus announced in Matthew 4 that the Kingdom of God was here, He was announcing that He, the King, had arrived on earth to regain His territory. The king of Portugal had to return to

Portugal to save his kingdom and authority there. God, as king, came in the person of Jesus to re-establish the earth as His unchallenged territory. Once He accomplished that, He returned to heaven, leaving us in charge of the colony. When Jesus ascended into heaven, He reinstated us as heirs to the Kingdom.

Paul explained this to the church in Ephesus in Ephesians 3.

> Ephesians 3:9-11
> *and to make plain to everyone the administration of this mystery, which for ages past was kept hidden in God, who created all things. His intent was that now, through the church, the manifold wisdom of God should be made known to the rulers and authorities in the heavenly realms, according to his eternal purpose that he accomplished in Christ Jesus our Lord.*

When Jesus walked this planet, most people missed that God Himself was among them, but that was clearly made known when He rose from the dead. The mystery was revealed to all who paid attention. Paul stated that the intention of Jesus coming to earth was that now, through the church, all spiritual authorities would be fully aware that the earth had been restored to the King. Adam lost a territory, and Jesus claimed it back.

THE PURPOSE OF THE CHURCH

When Jesus took the territory back, He wasn't just restoring it for Himself, but for us and our authority as well. The church has a vital role to play in the colony. Paul explained our authority and responsibility on this earth.

> 2 Corinthians 5:16-20
> *So from now on we regard no one from a worldly point of view. Though we once regarded Christ in this way, we do so no longer.*

> *Therefore, if anyone is in Christ, the new creation has come: The old has gone, the new is here! All this is from God, who reconciled us to himself through Christ and gave us the ministry of reconciliation: that God was reconciling the world to himself in Christ, not counting people's sins against them. And he has committed to us the message of reconciliation. We are therefore Christ's ambassadors, as though God were making his appeal through us.*

I love how Paul admitted, *"We once regarded Christ in this way."* I believe Paul admitted that he first saw Jesus from a worldly point of view. When he saw who Jesus was, and began to understand His Kingdom intentions in coming, Paul had a revelation of what really happened through Jesus' death and resurrection. He also began to realize who he was and his authority and responsibility on earth. We need to understand this, too.

Nehemiah anchored himself in his identity as part of God's chosen people. Knowing who he was gave him the boldness to present his requests to the king.

Paul gave us insight in 2 Corinthians 5 that because of Jesus we are more than just God's chosen people, we are His representatives here on earth. We are ambassadors of the King. This is no small thing. This doesn't just mean we have God's salvation and favor. It means we have a role and responsibility in His Kingdom, too.

The Webster's dictionary defines an ambassador as:

> : an official envoy
> especially : a diplomatic agent of the highest rank accredited to a foreign government or sovereign as the resident representative of his or her own government or sovereign or appointed for a special and often temporary diplomatic assignment.

An ambassador is the highest-ranked representative of his king in a territory. When Jesus was here, He was the highest-ranking representative because He is King. When He ascended to heaven, we became His ambassadors and are now the highest-ranking resident representatives of His Kingdom on earth! That's why Jesus said to His disciples in John 16:7, *"It is for your good that I am going away."* It didn't feel good to the disciples then because they missed their friend, mentor, and Savior. Later, they understood that when Jesus left, they gained authority on earth. It was for their betterment and ours, too!

WHAT IS AN AMBASSADOR?

A recent job description of a modern ambassador described the authority and responsibilities of an ambassador of the United States this way:

> Ambassadors for the United States mainly work to support U.S. interests in foreign countries and promote foreign policy strategies through international organizations. All ambassadors officially represent the U.S. government on behalf of the president in treaty negotiations, immigration discussions, foreign aid projects and humanitarian aid programs. Ambassadors supervise and lead all foreign service employees in the country where they work. As the chief executive of the U.S. embassy, an ambassador also monitors the activities of all U.S. personnel who work for any federal agency in their jurisdiction. The ambassador and her staff also aid Americans traveling in the country and provide security for U.S. citizens during emergencies and natural disasters. Ambassadors serve at the pleasure of the sitting president of the United States.[11]

Most of us prefer hierarchies and top-down organizational charts, which is not how God's Kingdom works. When the Apostle

Paul said, *"We are therefore Christ's ambassadors,"* he wasn't writing to the church leadership in Corinth. He was writing to the entire church. Therefore, the title of "ambassador" is not reserved for a few chosen and specially called people on the top of an organizational chart. It is the rank given to all of us, and with this position comes vital responsibilities.

As we can see in the summary of the job description for an American ambassador, they are responsible for representing the president and his government and interests. As ambassadors of the King of kings, we are accountable for representing Him on earth.

Before you say a resounding amen, I want you to feel the weight of that. This means we serve at His pleasure, not our own. This means we can't fit Him into our desired categories and make Him serve our wants and desires.

I've noticed a terrifying trend in today's church. This trend has always been there, as it is human nature. Of late, possibly because of the church's very public role in modern elections, I have noticed that Christians can make the Bible say what they want it to say. Both sides of the aisle can use scripture to justify their position on anything.

We can't ask God to be on our side. Whether we agree with His position or not, it is our job to be on His side. He is King.

When Joshua encountered the "angel of the Lord" in Joshua 5, he asked, *"Whose side are you on—ours or our enemies?"* To which the angel replied, *"Neither. I'm commander of God's army. I've just arrived."* Joshua fell, face to the ground, and worshiped. He asked, *"What orders does my Master have for his servant?"* [12]

We must be like Joshua and take the same posture on our faces in worship of our great King. Yes, we are His representatives, and we have authority, but He is King and, therefore, has the final say. It is not about Him being on our side. It's about us being on His. He doesn't take orders from us. We accept orders from Him.

It is the responsibility of an ambassador to represent their king. It is also the responsibility of an ambassador to represent their government "in treaty negotiations, immigration discussions, foreign aid projects and humanitarian aid programs."

We cannot miss the similarities between this job description and the instructions Jesus gave His disciples just before He ascended into heaven.

> Matthew 28:18-20
> *"All authority in heaven and on earth has been given to me.* (He already had full authority in heaven, but because of His death and resurrection, He took back all of the authority on earth) *Therefore go* (He commissioned us to go as His representatives) *and make disciples of all nations, baptizing them in the name of the Father and of the Son and of the Holy Spirit, and teaching them to obey everything I have commanded you. And surely I am with you always, to the very end of the age."*

Our role as ambassadors is to present God's invitation into His Kingdom to all nations. One could argue this is a form of "treaty negotiations and immigration discussions." According to Paul, this was not a suggestion from our King; it was a command, and therefore, we must obey.

> Romans 1:14-15
> *I am obligated both to Greeks and non-Greeks, both to the wise and the foolish. That is why I am so eager to preach the gospel also to you who are in Rome.*

Paul felt obligated to preach the gospel because he was an ambassador on assignment from his King, but preaching the gospel is not the only assignment Jesus gave. As we have already learned,

He gave the command to *"Love one another as I have loved you"*[13] and said that the righteous, which means those who would be in right standing with the King, would be those who ministered *"to the least of these."*[14] These instructions fall in line with the job description of an ambassador. Specifically, the ambassador's responsibilities include providing "foreign aid projects and humanitarian aid programs" and "security for citizens during emergencies and natural disasters." The similarities between the job description of an ambassador and the ones Jesus gave us are uncanny.

HIS ROLE AND OUR ROLE

As Christians, we must understand the Kingdom of God and His way of doing things. In particular, we need to understand His role as King and our role as citizens of heaven and ambassadors on earth. When we fail to understand the Kingdom, particularly our role and responsibilities, we tend to get weird and create bizarre theologies and religious practices. We take authority where we shouldn't and give away authority when we should take it.

Nehemiah anchored himself in Kingdom thinking. He knew where God had authority and where he had authority, and he walked that line perfectly. He recognized God as King, having the ultimate authority, yet didn't blame God for the state of his city. He acknowledged that Jerusalem was given to his people and was, therefore, in his realm of authority. An ambassador doesn't blame the king if the colony is in shambles. The colony is his territory to oversee. If it is in disrepair, then it is his responsibility to repair it. So, Nehemiah accepted personal and corporate responsibility, saying, *"I and my father's house have sinned."*[15]

Nehemiah also recognized that he did not have the authority over his earthly king. Even though he answered to a higher King, that did not mean he could violate the hierarchy of the system he lived under. Peter made this very clear in his epistle.

1 Peter 2:13-17 (ESV)
Be subject for the Lord's sake to every human institution, whether it be to the emperor as supreme, or to governors as sent by him to punish those who do evil and to praise those who do good. For this is the will of God, that by doing good you should put to silence the ignorance of foolish people. Live as people who are free, not using your freedom as a cover-up for evil, but living as servants of God. Honor everyone. Love the brotherhood. Fear God. Honor the emperor.

Understanding this principle of authority, Nehemiah got it right. He asked permission from his earthly king to fulfill his responsibility as an ambassador to the King of kings. He prayed to God and asked Him to grant him favor with the king of Persia. When God answered, and the king permitted him, Nehemiah gave credit where credit was due, saying, *"because the gracious hand of my God was on me, the king granted my requests."*[16]

When I read Nehemiah, I am both inspired and convicted. I am convicted because I don't think I would have responded as he responded. I would have been tempted to cast the blame on the king, or God, or anyone else I thought of. I wouldn't have accepted personal responsibility for my city. I would've asked God to fix the problem Himself, thereby missing a great opportunity. I seldom recognize where God's authority ends, and mine begins. I cast blame and abdicate responsibility. I see this in myself and don't think I'm the only one.

WHY DOESN'T GOD DO SOMETHING?

Why does God allow so much suffering in the world? Why doesn't God do away with evil? Why does God allow sickness to continue? Doesn't He care? Why doesn't God do something?

Have you asked one or more of these questions? Have you heard anyone else ask these same ones? I have! These questions indicate our ignorance of the Kingdom of God concerning our responsibility as ambassadors on earth.

We can't look at the suffering in the world and blame God. This is our territory. If the world is dark and getting darker, it's because we aren't being the light of the world Jesus told us to be in Matthew 5. If there is suffering, we must bring healing and peace.

An indication that we don't fully grasp the Kingdom of God as modern Christians is that we have common sayings like, "He's got the whole world in His hands." While our intention may be to comfort the suffering, this statement abdicates our responsibility. Statements like these not only fail to bring comfort to those suffering, but they can also confirm their feelings that God abandoned them, doesn't care enough about them, is a terrible manager, or, at the very minimum, has allowed the hardship to occur.

The earth is God's territory, but it is our jurisdiction. If suffering is left unchecked, it is not His abandonment; it's ours. He gave us the authority and responsibility here. We need to understand our territory, recognize our responsibilities, and take our job back.

CHAPTER EIGHT

BIG GOVERNMENT

Paul told the church in Corinth that, as Christians, they had been positioned as ambassadors tasked with representing the King and His government on the earth. This is a heavy responsibility. In order to represent our King well, we must know all we can about Him and His government.

Having grown up in the church and having attended Bible College, I have been taught about the nature and character of God, and rightfully so. To represent Him, we must know Him, not just about Him. However, we are also called to be His ambassadors, so we should also fully know and understand His government.

For some of you who have been Christians for a while, this might be the first time you have heard of God's government and your responsibility to know and represent it. As a pastor, I apologize for not teaching His government with more clarity. It is part of our responsibility as pastors and teachers to instruct people in the ways of God.

In this chapter, I will attempt to clarify the government of God as we see it laid out for us in the Bible and how the church taught it through the centuries. Hopefully, we will gain clarity and better understand our role and responsibilities within His government.

DOES GOD HAVE A GOVERNMENT?

Let's be honest, governments are not viewed favorably these days. Does God really operate with a government, too? How do we know? Isaiah prophesied the coming Messiah and King in Isaiah 9. This passage gets quoted every Christmas, but let's look at it again.

> Isaiah 9:6-7
> *For to us a child is born, to us a son is given, and the government will be on his shoulders. And he will be called Wonderful Counselor, Mighty God, Everlasting Father, Prince of Peace. Of the greatness of his government and peace there will be no end.*

Twice in these two short verses, the word government is used. The prophet said that when the King came, He would bring His government.

This reminds me, again, of the King of Portugal. When he fled Portugal in 1808, it was reported that he took his court to Brazil. The King didn't just go to Brazil on his own. He brought his government with him and established it there until 1821. When he returned to Portugal, his government returned with him.

The prophet proclaimed that Jesus would come to us as a child. He was prophesying that the King was coming to earth. Isaiah also clarified that He would bring His government with Him when He came. In verse 7, he stated that "His government" would not end, indicating that while the King might return to heaven, His government would remain here, without end.

Our God is the Creator, the Alpha and Omega, beginning and end. His rule will never end. Every Jew knew that. So, why did Isaiah need to make that point? He made this statement so that we would be clear that while the King would leave and return to heaven, His government would remain with us without end.

WHAT IS GOVERNMENT?

The dictionary defines a government as:

noun:

1. the political direction and control exercised over the actions of the members, citizens, or inhabitants of communities, societies, and states; direction of the affairs of a state, community, political administration:
   Government is necessary to the existence of civilized society.
2. the form or system of rule by which a state, community, is governed:
   monarchical government; episcopal government.
3. the governing body of persons in a state, community, administration.
4. a branch or service of the supreme authority of a state or nation, taken as representing the whole:
   a dam built by the government.
5. (in some parliamentary systems, as that of the United Kingdom)
   a. the particular group of persons forming the cabinet at any given time:
      The prime minister has formed a new government.
   b. the parliament along with the cabinet:
      The government has fallen.
6. direction; control; management; rule:
   the government of one's conduct.

To summarize, a government is the administrative body

responsible for executing the functions of governing, which include establishing order, administration, distribution, protection, maintenance, accountability, responsibility, and productivity.

The Greek word for government is kubernites, which means to steer, pilot, or act as a rudder. Therefore, government is the power given or derived to make and enforce laws for a particular territory.

Governing incorporates the concepts of both power and authority. These two elements must be in perfect balance for the government to succeed. Authority has to do with responsibility, while power has to do with ability. Power without legitimate authority is dictatorship and inevitably results in abuse, oppression, and destruction.[1]

This is why we, as believers, must clearly understand God's government and way of doing things. When the lines become blurred, and we exercise power where the King hasn't given us authority, the results are catastrophic and abusive. We have seen evidence of this abuse throughout church history.

In the same way, the results are no less deadly when we do not exercise our authority where we have been empowered to do so. We must live and act clearly and confidently in our authority *and* responsibilities. When we get it right, the entire world rejoices with the impact and is drawn to our King. He becomes irresistible. When we get it wrong, we misrepresent our King, and people get hurt.

WE WERE CREATED TO GOVERN

Mankind was made to govern. God created us that way. God first gave Adam and Eve a garden (a territory) to care for.

> Genesis 2:5-7
> *Now no shrub had yet appeared on the earth and no plant had yet sprung up, for the Lord God had not sent rain on the earth and there was no one to work the ground, but streams came up from*

the earth and watered the whole surface of the ground. Then the Lord God formed a man from the dust of the ground and breathed into his nostrils the breath of life, and the man became a living being.

God created us to take care of His creation on earth. He didn't send rain to the earth until He created man to care for the garden. God is not an irresponsible manager. He sets things in order and created us in His image to do the same thing.

Genesis 2:15
The Lord God took the man and put him in the Garden of Eden to work it and take care of it.

God created Adam and Eve to take care of the garden. When they sinned, they didn't lose heaven or a religion. They lost their territory. They lost their authority to govern the garden.

Jesus came as the new Adam, with the government on His shoulders, to re-establish His territory and set into place His government. Then, He commissioned the church to be the ambassadors, the leadership, of that territory.

God created us with the innate ability to govern. We crave power, not because we are sinful, but because it's in our DNA to rule. Within the lines of our authority, it is perfect and beautiful. Outside of those lines, it becomes laborious, dangerous, and abusive. Adam and Eve found that out when they sinned. They were removed from the garden and placed into the world without the authority to govern it. They still had the internal drive to govern and exercise power, so they worked, toiled, and felt the subsequent pains of their fallible human efforts. It wasn't long before the drive for power became abusive and deadly. Cain, the son of Adam and Eve, killed Abel, his brother, in the first power struggle.

God saw the destructive nature of mankind left to their own devices, so He pressed the reset button and started again with the flood and Noah. Then, God set up a temporary governing system with the tribes of Israel, establishing a Theocracy as their King and ruling through designated prophets. He even put into place a constitution known as the Law of Moses. The system worked with God at the top and when the people obeyed the established law. But the Israelites demanded their own system. They wanted to be like every other nation and have their own earthly king.

As I have said, the need to rule and govern is built into our DNA. We can't blame the Israelites for wanting to rule themselves. But that desire went against God's original governmental structure. God created the world to be His outpost, with Him as King. He designed us to rule and take care of this territory. Problems ensue when we rebel against that order, make ourselves king, and choose to self-govern.

God created gravity. It's a pre-established law of the earth. If people try to deny or ignore it, problems happen, and someone gets hurt. At the same time, God gave us tremendous freedom to rule within this pre-established law. That's how good a King He is. We have the latitude to create and invent ways to work around gravity. We can invent airplanes that defy gravity, but even an aircraft has to adhere to the law.

THE DANGER OF MAN-MADE GOVERNMENTS

Israel wanted to self-govern. God gave in to their request. He is not a dictator and knows this is our territory to rule.

> 1 Samuel 8:4-7
> *So all the elders of Israel gathered together and came to Samuel at Ramah. They said to him, "You are old, and your sons do not follow your ways; now appoint a king to lead us, such as all the*

other nations have." But when they said, "Give us a king to lead us," this displeased Samuel; so he prayed to the Lord. And the Lord told him: "Listen to all that the people are saying to you; it is not you they have rejected, but they have rejected me as their king."

There is always a possibility for a colony to rebel against its king and declare independence, as Brazil did to Portugal in 1822. The king, in return, could respond by squashing the rebellion with force or letting the colony go. When Israel demanded independence and the right to self-govern, Samuel wanted God to retaliate. God chose to let them go, but not before warning them of the consequences of their request.

1 Samuel 8:9-18

Now listen to them; but warn them solemnly and let them know what the king who will reign over them will claim as his rights." Samuel told all the words of the Lord to the people who were asking him for a king. He said, "This is what the king who will reign over you will claim as his rights: He will take your sons and make them serve with his chariots and horses, and they will run in front of his chariots. Some he will assign to be commanders of thousands and commanders of fifties, and others to plow his ground and reap his harvest, and still others to make weapons of war and equipment for his chariots. He will take your daughters to be perfumers and cooks and bakers. He will take the best of your fields and vineyards and olive groves and give them to his attendants. He will take a tenth of your grain and of your vintage and give it to his officials and attendants. Your male and female servants and the best of your cattle and donkeys he will take for his own use. He will take a tenth of your flocks, and you yourselves will become his slaves. When that day comes, you will cry out for relief from the king you have chosen, but the Lord will not answer you in that day."

Man's system of government is much different than God's. We are naturally selfish and sinful. Regardless of our intentions, we will inevitably make a mess because we will create systems that serve our self-interests.

No matter how hard we try to prevent corruption, power and control, human nature will always pull toward these things. The American forefathers wrote a stunning document in the form of the Constitution in an attempt to prevent the corruption of power they had just escaped. They intended to decentralize the authority by forming a democratic government with multiple checks and balances. However, even the best-intended constitutions eventually fall apart, and no matter the protections written into them, they will fail. We are witnessing it as we speak. We are who we are, and we can't run from our nature.

According to God, mankind's government will be about command, control, and coin. These three items are written into God's warning to the Israelites. Every man-made governmental system eventually comes down to these three.

Let's take a look at some of our man-made governmental systems. All of these were created with good intentions, but as you will see, all far desperately short.

Feudalism: Feudalism also known as the feudal system, combined the legal, economic, military, and cultural customs that flourished in Medieval Europe between the 9th and 15th centuries. It was broadly defined as a way of structuring society around relationships derived from holding land in exchange for service or labor.

Feudalism was built around the fundamental concepts of lords, vassals and fiefs. In broad terms, a lord was a noble who held land, a vassal was a person who was granted possession of the land by the lord, and the land was known as a fief. In exchange for the use of the fief and protection by the lord, the vassal would provide some sort of service to the lord. There were many varieties of feudal land tenure, consisting of military and non-military service. The obligations and corresponding rights between lord and vassal concerning the fief form the basis of the feudal relationship.

In other words, the lord was king because he owned the land. If you lived on his land, you were automatically in his kingdom and served him however he saw fit. The lord (which means owner) was responsible for caring for all the needs of those under their care.

In many cases, the lord or king would be kind and benevolent toward the people who lived and worked on his land. The people would be happy and would, in turn, serve well, thus making the land more productive and prosperous for the lord. This benevolence would also attract many more people to the land, thus expanding the kingdom.

However, on other occasions, the lord or king would not be so kind and would rule with fear, control, and abuse. The people would have to comply to survive. Eventually, the system broke down in the 12th century and was basically gone by the 16th century. Why? Well, eventually, people stopped wanting to be ruled and wanted to own their own land. It's the nature of human beings to want to own and rule. The power in this period becomes more personal.[2]

Dictatorship: A dictatorship is a form of government characterized by a single leader (dictator) or group of leaders that hold government power promised to the people. Typically, in a dictatorial regime, the leader of the country is identified with the title of dictator or "divine ruler;" although their formal title may more closely resemble something similar to leader. A common aspect that characterizes dictatorship is taking advantage of their strong personality, usually by suppressing the freedom of thought and speech of the masses, to maintain complete political and social supremacy and stability. Dictatorships generally employ political propaganda to decrease the influence of proponents of alternative governing systems.[3]

I don't think I need to explain the results of a dictatorship on a people and a nation. We have seen many examples of this system failing in recent history.

Communism: Communism is an excellent example of man trying to self-govern with the best intentions. On paper, communism attempts to remove the greed aspect of human nature by making all properties and ownership common. Individuals in a communist society don't own land or properties. The government owns all. This is an attempt to avoid the power struggles over land and to create a classless society. In theory, equalizing everyone in a society would make everyone happy. The actual results have proven the opposite.

Communism fails to take into account our human nature to own and rule. It also resulted in significant overreaches and abuses by a government without accountability. In many cases, leaders in a communist nation became dictators who led with fear and control.

Socialism: Socialism is the stepchild of communism in that it is another noble attempt to mitigate greed by creating social ownership. Socialism, however, varies in that it is an attempt to bring the government closer to the needs of the people. It attempts to control society for the benefit of society. It creates a big government with sweeping powers and a massive tax load on its citizens. It justifies this tax burden as a way to eliminate the poor in society. The result is a state with absolute power, and as is often said, absolute power corrupts absolutely.

Many socialists claim to have taken the foundation of their beliefs from the teachings of Jesus. They use Acts 4:35 as an example, which records that in the early church in Jerusalem, *"no one claimed that any of their possessions was their own."*

Again, there is a big difference between theory and practice. Socialism is still a man-made system and despite its best intentions, has proven throughout history to create unequivocal abuses of power.

Democracy: Democracy is a form of government in which the people have the authority to deliberate and decide legislation or to choose governing officials to do so. It is viewed by many people, including Christians worldwide, as the perfect government. The rule of the people, by the people, for the people is a fine idea. It is man's valiant attempt to escape the abuses of power and tyrannical rule.

Democracy has its roots in the writing of Greek philosophers. Plato wrote about democracy and called it the fairest of all constitutions, yet he also warned about its downfalls. According to him, equality brings power-seeking individuals motivated by personal gain. They can be highly corruptible, and this can eventually lead to tyranny.

This form of government is unstable and often lacks leaders with proper skills and morals. Plato saw democracy as potentially dangerous as it tends to motivate the poor against the wealthy rulers. It prioritizes wealth and property accumulation.[4]

As you can see, man makes valiant attempts to rule justly. And while it is in our nature to rule, we were not created to be "big-K-Kings." We were created to be ambassadors and "small-k-kings" under the authority of the King of kings. Under His authority, we have the power to rule righteously. Outside of His authority, we tend to abuse power excessively, leading to much pain and heartache.

This is the problem with the worldview. It is inherently self-seeking. The less internal government you have, the more external government you need.

Man-made governments tend to rule with command and control. Command and control are usually centered around power (who is in command) and coin (who controls the wealth). In contrast, the Kingdom of God rules differently.

GOD'S GOVERNMENT AND WAY OF DOING THINGS

God's Kingdom and government rule have two distinct elements: love and servant leadership. When I speak of God ruling with love, I'm not talking about the airy-fairy, feeling kind of love. I'm talking about the dying-to-self type of love.

The second component of His government is service. If you want to lead in His government, serve. If you want to be great, become the servant of all.

These two elements sound simple. They are, in theory, but they are anything but simple in everyday practice. Jesus told His disciples that they would have to *"take up their cross and die daily."* [5] He said this because it is our natural tendency to be like the Israelites and think that we can self-govern. Yet, we know we can't successfully self-govern without overstepping the boundaries of authority and power, which leads to abusive command, control, and greed.

We need to know how God's government works, and we need to know our place in it. We need to understand our power and authority and not get these out of order because when we do, we hurt many people and, ultimately, damage the very Kingdom we are called to advance and protect. There has been nothing more destructive and deadly throughout history than the abuse of power in the name of God.

We have already learned about some of those abuses in church history, and it is clear to see where our "forefathers" have sinned and missed the mark. Why is it necessary to learn the errors of the past? The Apostle Paul gave us the reason.

> 1 Corinthians 10:11-14 (Msg)
> *These are all warning markers—danger!—in our history books, written down so that we don't repeat their mistakes. Our positions in the story are parallel—they at the beginning, we at the end—and we are just as capable of messing it up as they*

> *were. Don't be so naive and self-confident. You're not exempt. You could fall flat on your face as easily as anyone else. Forget about self-confidence; it's useless. Cultivate God-confidence. No test or temptation that comes your way is beyond the course of what others have had to face. All you need to remember is that God will never let you down; he'll never let you be pushed past your limit; he'll always be there to help you come through it. So, my very dear friends, when you see people reducing God to something they can use or control, get out of their company as fast as you can.*

That is a very stern warning. When you see people reducing God to something they can use or control, run! That's precisely what Martin Luther did in 1517. But that doesn't mean human nature hasn't taken over again. Protestants and Catholics alike often try to self-govern, using God as a means to command and control people.

In Paul's own words, *"Don't be so naive and self-confident. You're not exempt. You could fall flat on your face as easily as anyone else."* I know I have. I have scars on my face to prove it. We all need to realize that we tend to repeat history. So, let's not be self-righteous, thinking we are exempt. But let us be confident in knowing who we are and know our King and His government.

Paul promised that *"God will never let you down, He'll always be there to help you come through it."* The key is always to stay close to the King. The closer to the King we get, the more Kingdom-like we will become. As Francois Fenelon said, "The Kingdom of God which is within us consists in our willing whatever God wills, always, in everything, and without reservation; and thus His Kingdom comes." The Kingdom is within. We just need to draw it out. And, with God's help, we can.

How can we quickly recognize when we are getting off track? How can we know when we aren't correctly balancing our authority and power? What does missing the mark look like today? And, what is its fruit?

We're going to answer these questions and more in the next chapter.

CHAPTER NINE

DON'T MOVE THE LAMPSTAND

When was the last time you started a brand-new job? Do you remember the excitement and nervousness you felt for your first shift? You were excited about the new beginning but nervous because you didn't know if you would do what was expected of you by your new boss.

Now imagine if your new boss invited you to sit with her as she conducted employee evaluations for seven current staff members. You would learn about the job, what is expected of an employee, and how your boss thinks. It'd be invaluable.

God allowed us to sit in on the performance evaluations of seven of the first churches in Revelation 2-3. These two chapters give insight into what's expected of a church in God's government. We see what is considered right and what is considered missing the mark. We also learn a great deal about how God thinks. Let's take a look at what we can learn from these chapters.

WHAT IS THE PURPOSE OF THE LAMPSTAND?

John gives us critical insight into the terminology he will use throughout the book of Revelation.

Revelation 1:20
The mystery of the seven stars that you saw in my right hand and of the seven golden lampstands is this: The seven stars are the angels of the seven churches, and the seven lampstands are the seven churches.

The metaphor of a lampstand, in reference to the church, is significant. John wrote the book of Revelation to the Jewish believers of the first-century church. As Jews who were raised to know and memorize the Torah, they would have immediately understood the lampstand to be a direct reference to the piece of furniture God commanded to be put in the Tabernacle. Besides God's presence, the lampstand was the only light source in the Tabernacle. The priest's primary job was ensuring the light on the lampstand never burned out.

The lampstand was positioned strategically across from the Table of Showbread in the Holy Place of the Tabernacle to do two things: be a light source and, in particular, to cast its light on the showbread. The symbolism cannot be missed. Jesus called Himself the Bread of Life in John 6:35. In using the lampstand metaphor; John stated that the church exists to shine a light into the darkness, specifically to illuminate Jesus so that the world can see Him and know Him.

Jesus used a similar analogy in Matthew 5.

Matthew 5:14-16
"You are the light of the world. A town built on a hill cannot be hidden. Neither do people light a lamp and put it under a bowl. Instead they put it on its stand, and it gives light to everyone in

the house. In the same way, let your light shine before others, that they may see your good deeds and glorify your Father in heaven."

The purpose of the church being the "light of the world" is to illuminate Jesus by doing "good deeds" before men. The seven letters to the seven churches in Revelation 2-3 were a report card on how they performed their duty as lampstands. Were they in the correct position, illuminating the right things? Everything about these churches, their teaching, practices, and their work, was evaluated for one reason: their effectiveness as God's light to their communities.

If you search long enough, you can find a host of intelligent leaders who have put their personal spin on why the church exists. I have read many contradicting opinions on how to do church or what the church should look like, but we are not looking for man's opinion on how the church should govern itself. We are looking for the King's opinion. We don't want to make the same mistake as the Israelites in Samuel's time and try to self-govern ourselves using a man-made system. We want to represent the King and His interests as He designed us to.

How does God want the church to govern? How does the church keep the lampstand in the proper position, lighting the right thing?

THE CHURCH OF EPHESUS

Let's see what insight we can discover from God's job evaluation of the churches in Revelation. We must remember that these were real churches with real people who lived in a real time. This is not metaphorical. This is real.

Revelation 2:1-7

"To the angel of the church in Ephesus write:

These are the words of him who holds the seven stars in his right

> *hand and walks among the seven golden lampstands. I know your deeds, your hard work and your perseverance. I know that you cannot tolerate wicked people, that you have tested those who claim to be apostles but are not, and have found them false. You have persevered and have endured hardships for my name, and have not grown weary. Yet I hold this against you: You have forsaken the love you had at first. Consider how far you have fallen! Repent and do the things you did at first. If you do not repent, I will come to you and remove your lampstand from its place. But you have this in your favor: You hate the practices of the Nicolaitans, which I also hate. Whoever has ears, let them hear what the Spirit says to the churches. To the one who is victorious, I will give the right to eat from the tree of life, which is in the paradise of God.*

The first evaluation was of the famous church in Ephesus. Paul wrote to this church in the book of Ephesians. Timothy eventually became the bishop or overseer of the Ephesian church. It played a crucial role in the early years of the Christian movement. Ephesus, at this time, had a population of over 250,000. It housed the Great Temple of Artemis, the center for the worship of the goddess Diana. It was also the commercial center of Asia Minor in the first century. Ephesus was significant to the broader culture at the time, and the city was also significant in the context of the ancient Christian world. The church became one of the most important influences in early Christianity and was known as the mother church in Asia Minor.

Each report begins with the words, "These are the words of…" and gives a brief one-sentence description of our King. This is invaluable information and provides incredible insight into who Jesus is. The report of Ephesus describes Jesus as the one who *"holds the seven stars in his right hand and walks among the seven golden lampstands."* As we learned in Revelation 1:20, the stars represent the angels, and the lampstands represent the churches. John is saying that Jesus is King of the heavens and on the earth. His authority is equal in both realms.

Proceeding this brief description of Jesus comes the "performance review" of the church itself. The review starts well, using words like "hard work" and perseverance. This was for a good reason. The Ephesians lived in a hostile culture. The church, at this time, was small and marginalized. They also had a reputation for causing problems (see Acts 19). Yet, the gospel spread rapidly in this incredibly dark place, transforming an entire region.

Then comes the "but." Yes, they were hard-working and persevered, but they had *"forsaken their first love."* New Testament Scholar N.T. Wright said, "It's easy to let this slip. It's easy to settle down into a vaguely comfortable existence which puts its own needs first and, sometimes, last as well. The Ephesian church needs to wake up, to remember how things used to be, to repent and get back on track."[1]

The Ephesian church had become complacent. That might be why Paul wrote to them this way in Ephesians 1.

> Ephesians 1:16-21 (Msg)
> *I ask—ask the God of our Master, Jesus Christ, the God of glory—to make you intelligent and discerning in knowing him personally, your eyes focused and clear, so that you can see exactly what it is he is calling you to do, grasp the immensity of this glorious way of life he has for his followers, oh, the utter extravagance of his work in us who trust him—endless energy, boundless strength! All this energy issues from Christ: God raised him from death and set him on a throne in deep heaven, in charge of running the universe, everything from galaxies to governments, no name and no power exempt from his rule.*

Paul refocused them on Jesus, pushing them to get their energy and passion from Him. How? By refocusing them on His Kingship and authority. This focus would then reflect on them and their authority. The idea of an ambassador of Christ isn't to generate light but to reflect light. We're to be like a solar-powered flashlight. Instead of operating through batteries or an internal power source, it must first receive light from the sun to give light. If it doesn't receive light, it has no light to give.

THE CHURCH OF SMYRNA

The second "performance review" was to the church in Smyrna.

> Revelation 2:8-11
> *"To the angel of the church in Smyrna write:*
> *These are the words of him who is the First and the Last, who died and came to life again. I know your afflictions and your poverty—yet you are rich! I know about the slander of those who say they are Jews and are not, but are a synagogue of Satan. Do not be afraid of what you are about to suffer. I tell you, the devil will put some of you in prison to test you, and you will suffer persecution for ten days. Be faithful, even to the point of death, and I will give you life as your victor's crown. Whoever has ears, let them hear what the Spirit says to the churches. The one who is victorious will not be hurt at all by the second death.*

The description ascribed to Jesus here is that He has ruled as King from the beginning and will rule to the end and is King because He died and rose again. Remember, this revelation caused the two disciples on the road to Emmaus to proclaim that the *"Lord is alive."* After the resurrection, Thomas declared, *"My Lord and my God."* The resurrection is the foundation of our faith and reveals to all that Jesus is truly King.

Smyrna was destroyed in 600 BC and rebuilt in 290 BC. Because of this history, Smyrna was known as a city that died and returned to life. John used their history as an opportunity to reiterate that Jesus is King and that His resurrection is evidence of His ultimate authority.

When Rome came to power, Smyrna quickly showed support. It was one of the first cities in Asia Minor to construct a temple to worship the emperor Caesar. In Smyrna, worshiping Caesar as Lord was a way of ensuring favor from Rome. It was viewed as patriotic, and refusing to worship Caesar was treacherous. Jesus' followers in Smyrna claimed Jesus as Lord, not Caesar, and they lost everything in return. Anyone who refused to worship Caesar was prohibited from working in the city. Therefore, the Christians were poor, ostracized, and abused. They knew their faith could cost them their lives.

They faced persecution from the Romans, but the Jews also persecuted them. One would think that because the Jews worshiped the same God, they would've defended the Christians against the Romans. Instead, they added to the persecution. Often, being stabbed in the back by someone who should have your back is the most challenging persecution to endure.

To summarize this review, the church in Smyrna was commended for not moving its lampstand. Despite the unimaginable pressure, they kept the King and His Kingdom as their ultimate priority and focus.

THE CHURCH OF PERGAMUM

The third "performance review" was to the church in Pergamum.

Revelation 2:12-17

To the angel of the church in Pergamum write:

These are the words of him who has the sharp, double-edged sword. I know where you live—where Satan has his throne. Yet

> *you remain true to my name. You did not renounce your faith in me, not even in the days of Antipas, my faithful witness, who was put to death in your city—where Satan lives. Nevertheless, I have a few things against you: There are some among you who hold to the teaching of Balaam, who taught Balak to entice the Israelites to sin so that they ate food sacrificed to idols and committed sexual immorality. Likewise, you also have those who hold to the teaching of the Nicolaitans. Repent therefore! Otherwise, I will soon come to you and will fight against them with the sword of my mouth. Whoever has ears, let them hear what the Spirit says to the churches. To the one who is victorious, I will give some of the hidden manna. I will also give that person a white stone with a new name written on it, known only to the one who receives it.*

Twice, God says that Satan lives and has his throne in Pergamum. It must've been a lovely place! Why did God have such strong opinions about it?

Pergamum was Asia's capital for almost 250 years and was considered by many as its greatest city. Its buildings towered 1,000 feet above the plain, projecting the image of a royal city. Like Smyrna, it was also the home of emperor worship, but it was the first temple dedicated to the worship of a living emperor (Caesar Augustus). God did not take kindly to a human elevating himself to the status of a god.

The Church in Pergamum remained faithful to Christ and His teachings even in a culture steeped in emperor worship and satanic practices. God commends them for remaining *"true to my name"* but rebukes them for allowing false doctrine to go unaddressed.

The comparison to *"the teaching of Balaam"* refers to an Old Testament prophet who led the Israelites astray with false teachings and into compromise.

The false doctrine that Jesus was most concerned about in

Pergamum was the teachings of the Nicolaitans, who were the followers of Nicolas, one of the first seven ordained by the apostles. They had a reputation for being prone to compromise and were said to live lives of unrestrained indulgence.

The references to Balaam and the Nicolaitians point to the same issue. Compromise. The big question addressed in this letter is, what do we do with sin? Do we handle it with grace or truth? The church in Pergamum did neither.

Grace and truth can seem like contradictions when they are two sides of the same coin. Grace enables us to be open to others, to love our enemies, to pray for those who persecute us, and to show authentic mercy and forgiveness to those who sin against us. But we must also relentlessly protect the truth of who Jesus is. Jesus alone is God and deserves our worship and allegiance. Any compromise must be resisted.

Jesus was full of grace and truth, hence the reference to the double-edged sword. Both sides were as sharp as the other. We are to be the same. When we move the lampstand to the position of shining a light on sin, to expose it in someone else, we are abusing our power and only using one side of the sword. We have not been given the authority to remove sin. Only God has that authority. We aren't to shine a light on sin as much as we are to use the lampstand to shine a light to illuminate a path to Jesus.

THE CHURCH OF THYATIRA

The "performance reviews" continued:

Revelation 2:18-29

To the angel of the church in Thyatira write:

These are the words of the Son of God, whose eyes are like blazing fire and whose feet are like burnished bronze. I know your deeds, your love and faith, your service and perseverance, and that you are now doing more than you did at first. Nevertheless, I have this against you: You tolerate that woman Jezebel, who calls herself a prophet. By her teaching she misleads my servants into sexual immorality and the eating of food sacrificed to idols. I have given her time to repent of her immorality, but she is unwilling. So I will cast her on a bed of suffering, and I will make those who commit adultery with her suffer intensely, unless they repent of her ways. I will strike her children dead. Then all the churches will know that I am he who searches hearts and minds, and I will repay each of you according to your deeds. Now I say to the rest of you in Thyatira, to you who do not hold to her teaching and have not learned Satan's so-called deep secrets, 'I will not impose any other burden on you, except to hold on to what you have until I come.' To the one who is victorious and does my will to the end, I will give authority over the nations— that one 'will rule them with an iron scepter and will dash them to pieces like pottery'— just as I have received authority from my Father. I will also give that one the morning star. Whoever has ears, let them hear what the Spirit says to the churches.

Thyatira was a blue-collar, labor town. It was built upon trades, guilds and crafts. Trade unions dominated society. They had monthly meals and a strong pull on members. In addition, each union had a Greek god associated with it. Faithful worship was meant to ensure the prosperity of the trade. Christians who refused to participate in these ceremonies faced isolation and suffered economically.

The members of this church would have related to the bronze feet analogy since bronze making was prominent in Thyatira. However, they also needed to understand that Jesus saw all things. Jesus claims to have eyes of blazing fire, making it clear that His sight could pierce through the cloud of confusion and hiding. Jesus saw those doing well and needing affirmation, as well as those whose sin caused further separation.

Thyatira was a difficult city in which to be a Christian. So much of the commerce and government in the ancient world was tied to pagan worship. In Thyatira, it was explicitly tied to the sun god Apollo. This seemed to have enticed them to compromise and allow sexually immoral behaviour to spread in the church. These acts came through a false prophet whom God compared to Jezebel, the controlling wife of King Ahab, who brought immorality to Israel when she was queen.

The Church in Thyatira seemed split: some needed a strong warning, while others received affirmation for their faithfulness. They were commended for their sense of true dedication. However, they had compromised in critical areas; many lived licentious lives and ate food sacrificed to idols (they chose idolatry).

The main point Jesus tried to make to this church was regarding control. Those who compromised felt like they could control their own destinies. They were reminded that the King sees all and will reward or punish them according to their deeds.

THE CHURCH OF SARDIS

God continues evaluating the churches in chapter 3.

Revelation 3:1-6

To the angel of the church in Sardis write:

These are the words of him who holds the seven spirits of God and the seven stars. I know your deeds; you have a reputation of being alive, but you are dead. Wake up! Strengthen what remains and is about to die, for I have found your deeds unfinished in the sight of my God. Remember, therefore, what you have received and heard; hold it fast, and repent. But if you do not wake up, I will come like a thief, and you will not know at what time I will come to you. Yet you have a few people in Sardis who have not soiled their clothes. They will walk with me, dressed in white, for they are worthy. The one who is victorious will, like them, be dressed in white. I will never blot out the name of that person from the book of life, but will acknowledge that name before my Father and his angels. Whoever has ears, let them hear what the Spirit says to the churches.

Sardis does not exist anymore. In fact, of all seven churches, Sardis and Laodicea are the only cities that don't still exist today. However, Sardis had a rich history that included power, wealth, and prominence (to the point of arrogance). It was the capital city of the ancient kingdom of Lydia, strategically located on the communications route between Ephesus, Smyrna and Pergamum. It was famous for affluence and creative culture, such as arts and crafts, and was the first to mint gold and silver into coins.

In AD 17, an earthquake destroyed the city. Rome sent relief aid, but the city was saddled with debt and never recovered.

The message of this review was a warning of the dangers of complacency that often occurs when we become wealthy and self-reliant. We tend to feel less of a dependence on God when we believe we can supply our own needs. God warned them not to allow their current wealth and security to fool them. It wasn't going to last. All kingdoms end eventually, except the Kingdom of God. This is why Jesus mentioned that He would not blot out their names. He promised that even though the city's name would be blotted out, those who belonged to the everlasting Kingdom would remain forever.

The description given of God to this church was that He "*holds the seven spirits.*" The number seven is used in the Bible to signal completeness. Therefore, scholars believe the term "*seven spirits of God*" refers to the Holy Spirit. John Stott writes, "So Jesus reminds the Church of Sardis that…Christ has the Holy Spirit…it is He who can animate our dead works and make them pulsate with life. He can rescue a dying Church and make it a living force in the community."[2]

THE CHURCH OF PHILADELPHIA

The following review was to the church in Philadelphia. No, not the one in Pennsylvania.

> Revelation 3:7-13
> *To the angel of the church in Philadelphia write:*
> *These are the words of him who is holy and true, who holds the key of David. What he opens no one can shut, and what he shuts no one can open. I know your deeds. See, I have placed before you an open door that no one can shut. I know that you have little strength, yet you have kept my word and have not denied my name. I will make those who are of the synagogue of Satan, who claim to be Jews though they are not, but are liars—I will make them come and fall down at your feet and acknowledge that I have loved you. Since you have kept my command to endure patiently, I will also keep you from the hour of trial that is going to come on the whole world to test the inhabitants of the earth. I am coming soon. Hold on to what you have, so that no one will take your crown. The one who is victorious I will make a pillar in the temple of my God. Never again will they leave it. I will write on them the name of my God and the name of the city of my God, the new Jerusalem, which is coming down out of heaven from my God; and I will also write on them my new name. Whoever has ears, let them hear what the Spirit says to the churches.*

Philadelphia was founded to be a center of Greek culture and language, an outpost for spreading Hellenism to the regions of Lydia and Phrygia. Leather and textile businesses provided much income to the city and benefited from its location at the juncture of several important trade routes. This strategic location earned the city the title "Gateway to the East."

In AD 17, a powerful earthquake hit the city, causing significant damage, and the aftershocks continued for over 20 years. The city was eventually rebuilt through financial aid from Caesar Tiberius. Despite Tiberius acting as the city's savior, the church was reminded that Jesus had the keys and ultimately opened and closed doors. Tiberius might be king, but Jesus was the King of kings.

Philadelphia is one of only two churches in Revelation that received no rebuke or correction (the other is Smyrna). Believers in Philadelphia faced persecution regularly, much of it from the Jewish population of the city. Like Smyrna, the opposition was brutal in that Christ referred to the fanatical Jews as "the synagogue of Satan." Ouch!

Amid the severe persecution and opposition, and in light of His return, Jesus offered comfort to His followers in Philadelphia. He encouraged them to *"Hold onto what you have so that no one will take your crown."*

The King of kings is a king-maker. Ultimately, He made Tiberius king but also crowned the believers as kings, calling them sons and joint heirs with Him. Tiberius would one day relinquish his crown, but the believers would never lose theirs.

THE CHURCH OF LAODICEA

The last review was for a church in Laodicea.

> Revelation 3:14-22
> *To the angel of the church in Laodicea write:*
> *These are the words of the Amen, the faithful and true witness, the ruler of God's creation. I know your deeds, that you are neither cold nor hot. I wish you were either one or the other! So, because you are lukewarm—neither hot nor cold—I am about to spit you*

> *out of my mouth. You say, 'I am rich; I have acquired wealth and do not need a thing.' But you do not realize that you are wretched, pitiful, poor, blind and naked. I counsel you to buy from me gold refined in the fire, so you can become rich; and white clothes to wear, so you can cover your shameful nakedness; and salve to put on your eyes, so you can see. Those whom I love I rebuke and discipline. So be earnest and repent. Here I am! I stand at the door and knock. If anyone hears my voice and opens the door, I will come in and eat with that person, and they with me. To the one who is victorious, I will give the right to sit with me on my throne, just as I was victorious and sat down with my Father on his throne. Whoever has ears, let them hear what the Spirit says to the churches.*

Jesus is called *the Amen* because he is the One who confirmed all of God's promises (2 Corinthians 1:20). Jesus is the faithful and true witness because His testimony is entirely trustworthy, accurate, and reliable. Jesus is the ruler of God's creation because, through His power, all things were created.

Again, the point is clear. Jesus is King.

Laodicea was an extremely wealthy city. The people prided themselves on their financial independence. The city was so arrogant that its leadership refused Roman financial aid after an earthquake devastated it in 60 AD. Even the church boasted of its wealth and independence. *"You say, I am rich; I have acquired wealth and do not need a thing."* But Jesus called them wretched, poor and pitiful. It is alarming that the people of Laodicea didn't see themselves as Jesus did.

Although financially strong, the city had a significant weakness—its water supply. The waters of the nearby Lycus River were undrinkable, so Laodicea had to receive its water through aqueducts built by the Romans. Because the freshwater sources were so far away, the water they received was lukewarm by the time the cold water arrived from Colossae or the hot water from the springs in Hierapolis. This fact makes Jesus' point of a lukewarm church so much more poignant.

WHAT DOES A LUKEWARM CHURCH LOOK LIKE?

The emphasis on the lukewarm church sums up the rest of the performance reviews. What does a lukewarm church look like? What happens when we miss the mark? What happens when we instill our own government and reject God's government? What happens when we don't balance authority and power correctly? And what happens when we don't fully grasp the Kingdom of God?

1. We create churches that become *complacent* and lose their passion for Jesus.
2. We create churches that become *compassionless* and ignore the hurting and hopeless.
3. We create churches that *compromise* and are no longer concerned about holiness.
4. We create churches that *command* obedience instead of leading people with grace.
5. We create churches that *control* their surroundings to the degree that they get distracted by their methods and lose their focus on the mission.
6. We create churches that are distracted by *coin* and are more focused on looking good than on doing good.
7. We create churches that are more *concerned* about comfort and focus more on the needs of those inside the walls than those outside.

The Kingdom of God and His government is about love and service. Christendom, the earthly kingdom of the church, is complacent, compassionless, compromising, command and control, and focused on comfort and coin.

The Christendom church tends to create weird theologies. We're going to take a look at some of those theologies in the next chapter.

CHAPTER TEN

IDENTITY CRISIS

To say that our society is experiencing an identity crisis might be the understatement of the century. According to research done by Appalachian State University, there are "Big 8 Identities." They explain their research this way: "The "Big 8" comprises eight major identities that help us understand *who we are and where we come from. While this list is not all-encompassing, it allows us to explore some of our social group memberships–many (but not all) of which we are born into. Understanding who we are and who others are helps us honor human dignity and create authentically inclusive spaces.*"

The study goes on to list the eight identities and gives a brief explanation of each. The eight identities are:

1. Age
2. Ability: This identity is about the diverse array of differences in physical, mental, cognitive, developmental, learning, and/or emotional make-up. It also includes mental health and the impact of social experiences, such as trauma and surviving

abuse.

3. Race
4. Ethnicity: While race classifies people based on perceived physical characteristics, ethnicity relates more to culture, such as sharing a common language, ancestry, national origin, and/or a variety of cultural beliefs.
5. Gender: A person's deep seated felt-sense of who they are. Gender is different from sex in that sex is generally identified with one's anatomy. Examples of sex are female, male, intersex (having a combination of female and male parts).
6. Sexual Orientation: A person's sexual, emotional, romantic, and/or affectional attractions, not necessarily dependent on behavior.
7. Socioeconomic status: This category is commonly conceptualized as one's social standing in society based on income, wealth, or poverty. It is often used interchangeably with social class, but social class includes additional factors, such as a combination of education, income, occupation, lifestyle, and family background.
8. Religion[1]

The list is eight, but even in their explanations, they added two more that I can see: sex and social class. It goes without saying, but these eight categories can be broken down into enormous subcategories. For example, I was curious to see how big the subcategory of gender has become. According to healthline.com, at the time of this writing, 68 terms describe gender identity and expression.

Sixty-eight!

They go on to say, "Many people grew up with a simplistic idea of gender and sex: that there are two sexes, male and female, that "match" with two genders, man and woman. In reality, neither gender nor sex is binary."[2]

I don't bring this up to anger you or create a debate on these issues. My only intention is to highlight how serious the global identity crisis is and suggest that this crisis, in large part, is our fault as Christians. I and my fathers have sinned.

It is human nature to create a domain to rule. As we have already discovered, we were created by God to rule. When blinded to our Kingdom identity, we naturally create our own kingdoms and identities.

THE RELIGIOUS IDENTITY CRISIS

Investigating the religious category on ASU's list of eight is more alarming than the gender category. Did you know that there are over 4000 recognized religions in the world today? That's over 4000 different versions of how mankind can get to God. When we become unclear about what to believe, we inevitably try to make our own way.

We can break the religion category down into even more subcategories. Christianity is only one of 4000 different religions in the world today, and within Christianity itself, there are an estimated 45,000 different denominations. Forty-five thousand little-k-kingdoms all claiming to serve the Big-K-Kingdom. Meanwhile, we criticize the world's struggle with identity!

Jesus warned us about this. His passionate prayer in John 17 was about the unity of His followers.

John 17:9-11 (NASB)

I ask on their behalf; I do not ask on behalf of the world, but on the behalf of those whom You have given Me, because they are Yours; and all things that are Mine are Yours, and Yours are Mine; and I have been glorified in them. I am no longer going to be in the world; and yet they themselves are in the world, and I am coming to You. Holy Father, keep them in Your name, the name which You have given Me, so that they may be one just as We are.

Did you notice that Jesus didn't pray for world peace? He didn't ask for unity in the world. He knows that the lost will act lost. He had higher expectations for His church. He prayed that we would be one.

One. Not 45,000. Why?

John 17:20-21 (NASB)
I am not asking on behalf of these alone, but also for those who believe in Me through their word, that they may all be one; just as You, Father, are in Me and I in You, that they also may be in Us, so that the world may believe that You sent Me.

Just in case we might have thought that He was just praying for His disciples, no, He included all of us in His prayer, too. Twice, He prayed that we, His followers, would be one. He didn't pray that we would be right. He prayed that we would be one. To me, this indicates that it is more important to be one than it is to be right. That's not my opinion; that's the opinion and prayer of our King.

Why? Because according to Jesus, our unity would serve as the major beacon illuminating Jesus as King to the world.

Matthew 5:14-16 (NASB)
You are the light of the world. A city set on a hill cannot be hidden; nor do people light a lamp and put it under a basket, but on the lampstand, and it gives light to all who are in the house. Your light must shine before people in such a way that they may see your good works, and glorify your Father who is in heaven.

I wonder if the basket that hides the light of the world is our denominational mini-kingdoms and castles? We are intent as human beings to rule ourselves and select our own kings, and we do so by creating labels, identities, and camps that we can belong to. We build castles that we can rule. We weren't created to build castles but to build the Kingdom.

So, how did we come to this place? How did we create 45,000 castles flying 45,000 different flags claiming to be of the same Kingdom? Why are we so intent on creating labels, and what do we do about them?

WHAT IS A CHRISTIAN?

Did you know that the early Church never called themselves Christians? Jesus never actually gave a name to His followers. A label wasn't necessary.

In the Bible, the title most often used was "saints." The Greek word for saints is *hagios* which means "consecrated to God, holy, sacred, pious." The word is almost always used in the plural—"saints." This reflects the individual and the connection to a group of people set apart for the King and His Kingdom.

The term Christian was given to the church in Acts 11:26, *"and the disciples were first called Christians in Antioch."* Notice it says they were first *called* Christians. It wasn't a name they gave themselves. It was a name that the people in Antioch gave them.

Why?

Creating identities, categories, and labels isn't a new thing. Antioch was a multicultural city and was referred to as "all the world in one city." The city itself was designed to divide each race and group of people into their own areas, with actual walls constructed in the center of the city to separate them.

Along came the Jesus followers. They were inclusive and regularly crossed the divides. The city's people were uncomfortable with a group growing in their city without a label. They gave them a label that stuck, calling them Christians.

I don't think it is a coincidence that they were labeled Christian in the same chapter as Peter's controversial report to the leaders in Jerusalem. His report was controversial because he had crossed a significant line.

What line did he cross? He ate with Gentiles. Imagine, the labels were so strong that you couldn't even share a meal with another race.

While it's easy to criticize this thinking and classify it as extreme racism, we need to be careful. We tend to do similar things today. We are often reluctant to associate with those in other camps. We might not be divided by race, but we divide over labels. Republicans don't mix with Democrats. Conservatives won't tolerate Liberals. The Straight won't be seen with the LGTBQ2+. I could go on and on and on.

If we are beyond this immaturity, we should be beyond unfriending someone on social media who is from another camp or who disagrees with us. It's part of the societal norm to divide into categories. This is not new.

In Antioch, the Jesus followers stood out in the city precisely because they didn't fit into just one camp. So, they were given their own label.

PAUL REBUKES PETER

We are given remarkable insight into how important it was to the early church that Christians not fall into the same trap of labeling and dividing into camps as society did. In Galatians 2, the Apostle Paul publicly rebukes Peter for compromising in this way.

> Galatians 2:11-16 (Msg)
> *Later, when Peter came to Antioch, I had a face-to-face confrontation with him because he was clearly out of line. Here's the situation. Earlier, before certain persons had come from*

> *James, Peter regularly ate with the non-Jews. But when that conservative group came from Jerusalem, he cautiously pulled back and put as much distance as he could manage between himself and his non-Jewish friends. That's how fearful he was of the conservative Jewish clique that's been pushing the old system of circumcision. Unfortunately, the rest of the Jews in the Antioch church joined in that hypocrisy so that even Barnabas was swept along in the charade. But when I saw that they were not maintaining a steady, straight course according to the Message, I spoke up to Peter in front of them all: "If you, a Jew, live like a non-Jew when you're not being observed by the watchdogs from Jerusalem, what right do you have to require non-Jews to conform to Jewish customs just to make a favorable impression on your old Jerusalem buddies?" We Jews know that we have no advantage of birth over "non-Jewish sinners." We know very well that we are not set right with God by rule-keeping but only through personal faith in Jesus Christ. How do we know? We tried it—and we had the best system of rules the world has ever seen! Convinced that no human being can please God by self-improvement, we believed in Jesus as the Messiah so that we might be set right before God by trusting in the Messiah, not by trying to be good.*

Why did Paul feel the need to go public with this rebuke? Was it to position himself above Peter? Absolutely not. That would counter his character and everything else we know of Paul. Calling Peter out in public was harsh, but the future of the faith was at stake.

Where there is division, the Kingdom of God brings unity. Where there is brokenness, the Kingdom brings healing. In his behavior, Peter was directly contradicting the message of the Gospel. People would find it easy to discredit the message because it seemed no different than anything else.

We were first called Christians because the believers in Antioch were different; they modeled unity and refused to separate people into various camps. Are we living up to our given name? Can we show the world a vision of a community with no divides? Do our churches look any different than the world? Do our hearts? Are we living up to the vision of the Kingdom?[3]

Galatians 3:28
There is neither Jew nor Gentile, neither slave nor free, nor is there male and female, for you are all one in Christ Jesus.

Colossians 3:11
Here there is no Gentile or Jew, circumcised or uncircumcised, barbarian, Scythian, slave or free, but Christ is all, and is in all.

WHEN WE GET IT WRONG

Did you know that a revival of Hinduism began because a Christian violated this principle of the Kingdom?

One Sunday morning, Mahatma Gandhi decided to visit one of the Christian churches in Calcutta. He had just read the gospels and was intrigued by Jesus. As he walked up to the entrance of the church building, the ushers stopped him at the door. He was told he was not welcome, nor would he be permitted to attend this particular church as it was for high-caste Indians and whites only. He was neither high caste nor was he white. Because of the rejection, Gandhi turned his back on Christianity.[4]

He later wrote, "I reject any religious doctrine that does not appeal to reason and is in conflict with morality... God did not create men with the badge of superiority or inferiority; no scripture which labels a human being an inferior or untouchable because of his or her birth can command our allegiance. It is denial of God and Truth which is God."

He was famously quoted as saying, "I like your Christ, but not your Christianity."

Gandhi said of Jesus, "Jesus expressed as no other could, the spirit and will of God. It is in this sense that I see him and recognize as the Son of God. And because the life of Jesus has the significance and the transcendency to which I have alluded, I believe that he belongs not solely to Christianity but to the entire world, to all races and people. It matters little under what flag, name or doctrine they may work, profess a faith or worship a God inherited from their ancestors."

It seems like Gandhi understood the Kingdom of God more than most Christians. On seeing a painting of the crucified Christ in Rome, he remarked, "What would not I have given to be able to bow my head before the living image of Christ crucified. I saw there at once that nations like individuals could only be made through the agony of the cross and in no other way. Joy comes not out of infliction of pain on others but out of pain voluntarily borne by oneself."[5]

This segregation and divisive behavior has plagued the church since the very beginning, to the point where we now have 45,000 different denominations. We have divided over theologies, doctrines, power grabs, corruption, and more.

There were sects of the early church, like the Nicolatians in the first century, as we saw listed in Revelations 2 and 3, who are said to have propagated sexual immorality as part of Christianity. They claimed it was because Jesus freed them from the archaic law of Moses. God and the early church rejected this sect.

Then, there were the Arians in the third and fourth centuries. This controversy impacted most church members—from simple believers, priests, and monks to bishops, emperors, and members of Rome's imperial family. Two Roman emperors, Constantius II and Valens, became Arians or Semi-Arians. This sect started with Arius, a pupil of Lucian of Antioch. Arius taught that God the Father and the Son of God did not always exist together eternally. Emperor Constantine summoned the First Council of Nicaea, which defined the fundamental doctrines of Christianity; these definitions served to refute the questions posed by Arians."[6]

THE GREAT SCHISM

You know there is a problem with unity in the church when history records an event as the Great Schism. In 1054, the Eastern Orthodox split from the Roman Catholic Church. A succession of theological disputes between the Greek East and Latin West preceded the formal split in 1054. Prominent among these were the following the procession of the Holy Spirit, whether leavened or unleavened bread should be used during communion (seriously), and the bishop of Rome's claim to universal jurisdiction (having one Pope).[7]

There was another "schism" known as the Western Schism. It was a split within the Catholic Church that lasted from 1378 to 1417, during which both of the bishops residing in Rome and Avignon claimed to be the true pope and were joined by a third line of Pisan popes in 1409. The schism was driven by personalities and political allegiances, with the Avignon papacy closely associated with the French monarchy. This primarily political battle is said to have significantly damaged the prestige of the church's view of the Pope and his office.[8]

Professor MacCulluch, from Oxford, said that despite the handful of schisms, the Catholic Church successfully suppressed other potential Christian offshoots "partly by sustained persecution [including] actual military expeditions against some labeled heretics, but then also a new system of enquiries into people's beliefs, called inquisitions. With the backing of secular rulers, heretics might be burned at the stake or forced into denying their beliefs"[9]

Isn't that comforting? The church stymied off further splits for a season by using fear and violence. That is, of course, until the great Protestant Reformation in 1517.

DENOMINATIONALISM

We've already talked a lot about the reformation. Still, it is worth bringing up again because, after that, there was an explosion in the number of denominations beginning in 1534, when King Henry VIII started the Church of England. Christopher West, a doctoral student of ancient Christianity and medieval studies at Yale University, said that King Henry "wanted to establish the political autonomy of England, and one way to do that was religious autonomy from Rome." That, and he also famously wanted a divorce that the Catholic Church refused to grant.[10]

By the 17th century, the contemporary word "denomination" began to be used to describe religious offshoots. Michelle Sanchez, an associate professor of theology at Harvard Divinity School, said, "Protestants had used scripture to critique the Roman Catholic Church, claiming that any believer could read scripture and have a personal relationship with God. But then, the obvious problem emerged: Whose interpretation of scripture was the right one?"[11]

As believers debated the scriptures and sacraments, churches formed and split based on myriad Biblical interpretations, ways of worship and organizational structures. From these debates, denominations, such as the Presbyterians, Mennonites, Baptists and Quakers, among others, took root.[12] And here we are, 45,000 denominations later. A far cry from the prayer Jesus prayed.

SO WHAT DO WE DO NOW?

What can be done? Do we just throw our hands up, hopeless, and move on? Do we pray about it? Or do we survey the state of our land and, like Nehemiah, accept personal and corporate responsibility? "I and my fathers have sinned?"

And like Nehemiah, what if we surveyed the land and instead of getting overwhelmed and making excuses as to why we are in no position to do anything about it, what if we anchored ourselves in our Kingdom identity, rolled our sleeves up and went to work rebuilding?

We can't dissolve 45,000 denominations into one. But, what we can do is repent if we have acted like Peter and have personally contributed to the divides. We can heed the words of Paul again in 1 Corinthians 10.

1 Corinthians 10:11-14 (Msg)
These are all warning markers—danger!—in our history books, written down so that we don't repeat their mistakes. Our positions in the story are parallel—they at the beginning, we at the end—and we are just as capable of messing it up as they were. Don't be so naive and self-confident. You're not exempt. You could fall flat on your face as easily as anyone else. Forget about self-confidence; it's useless. Cultivate God-confidence. No test or temptation that comes your way is beyond the course of what others have had to face. All you need to remember is that God will never let you down; he'll never let you be pushed past your limit; he'll always be there to help you come through it. So, my very dear friends, when you see people reducing God to something they can use or control, get out of their company as fast as you can.

Interestingly, Paul seems to be encouraging a split, saying, "*get out of their company as fast as you can.*" The truth is that some splits are necessary and healthy. Martin Luther's splitting from a corrupt and controlling church was necessary. In the case of Gandhi, I wish he had met other Christians in another Kingdom-minded church who could have shown him love and acceptance as Christ would have.

What am I saying? If you are part of a group that encourages division, leave. We were not created to build castles. We were made to build the Kingdom. But, when you leave, do so with the Kingdom in mind, not your selfish desires and personal preferences. When we leave because of personal preference, we are wrong. That ultimately damages the Kingdom and does not have a Kingdom mindset.

Paul instructed us to maintain a Kingdom mindset during disagreements in Romans 12.

> Romans 12:9-21
> *Love must be sincere. Hate what is evil; cling to what is good. Be devoted to one another in love. Honor one another above yourselves. Never be lacking in zeal, but keep your spiritual fervor, serving the Lord. Be joyful in hope, patient in affliction, faithful in prayer. Share with the Lord's people who are in need. Practice hospitality. Bless those who persecute you; bless and do not curse. Rejoice with those who rejoice; mourn with those who mourn. Live in harmony with one another. Do not be proud, but be willing to associate with people of low position. Do not be conceited. Do not repay anyone evil for evil. Be careful to do what is right in the eyes of everyone. If it is possible, as far as it depends on you, live at peace with everyone. Do not take revenge, my dear friends, but leave room for God's wrath, for it is written: "It is mine to avenge; I will repay," says the Lord. On the contrary: "If your enemy is hungry, feed him; if he is thirsty, give him something to drink. In doing this, you will heap burning coals on his head." Do not be overcome by evil, but overcome evil with good.*

What if all of us just lived these thirteen verses out? It would be a game-changer. And, I believe the world would sit up and take notice, just like the citizens of Antioch did when they called a group who refused to divide Christian–or Christ-like. They were called that, not because what they taught seemed 'right,' but because how they lived seemed unusual and the most like their King.

The only ones who need to identify themselves by a label are the ones who don't know their Kingdom identity. We are not Catholic or Protestant, Baptist or Pentecostal. We are sons and daughters of the King, joint heirs with Him, and ambassadors of His Kingdom. Let's be wary of labels; be intent on building the Kingdom of God and not settle for building castles.

> Ephesians 1:20-23 (Msg)
> *All this energy issues from Christ: God raised him from death and set him on a throne in deep heaven, in charge of running the universe, everything from galaxies to governments, no name and no power exempt from his rule. And not just for the time being, but forever. He is in charge of it all, has the final word on everything. At the center of all this, Christ rules the church. The church, you see, is not peripheral to the world; the world is peripheral to the church.*

The world is peripheral to the church. I believe one of the reasons the world is experiencing an identity crisis is because the church is. If we would stop dividing, I think the world would follow suit.

In my time researching church history, something has stood out to me. With all of the divisions and schisms in church history, there seem to be significant gaps in time where there were no divides. I also noticed, and I'm sure you did, too, that since the Reformation, there has been a significant increase in separations. We briefly touched on a potential reason for this, but I am curious to discover if there is more to it than what we can see on the surface.

Did the focus of the church change? Is it a heart issue or a structural one? Did the activities and practices of the church change? I'm not looking for answers to these questions in small pockets of the church. I want to take a birds-eye view of the global church. Is there a general cause for the increase in division?

We will look at these questions in the next section of this book. We are also going to take the third position of Nehemiah. He didn't pray for a solution; he asked God for the opportunity to *be* the solution.

SECTION THREE

BE THE SOLUTION

CHAPTER ELEVEN

ABDICATED RESPONSIBILITIES

Today, those outside Christianity have a clearer understanding of what the church stands against than what it stands for. If we were to poll the general public and ask what they think the church does, the majority of the time, the first thing that would come out of their mouth is something we stand against.

They would list things like our stance against homosexuality, abortion, sex before marriage, or even our politics. They would be hard-pressed to know what the church stands *for* and are generally clueless about what we *do*. This wasn't always the case.

1 John 2:3-6
By this we know that we have come to know Him, if we keep His commandments. The one who says, "I have come to know Him," and does not keep His commandments, is a liar, and the truth is not in him; but whoever follows His word, in him the love of God has truly been perfected. By this we know that we are in Him: the one who says that he remains in Him ought, himself

also, walk just as He walked. Beloved, I am not writing a new commandment to you, but an old commandment which you have had from the beginning; the old commandment is the word which you have heard.

The religious often assume the word "commandments" directly refers to the Mosaic law, particularly the Ten Commandments. They see the Bible as a rule book, a list of do's and don'ts, and focus specifically on the don'ts. So, *"keeping His commandments"* means to not 'sin.' It means to not take the Lord's name in vain. It means not to lie, cheat, steal, or commit adultery. It means to not have sex outside of marriage, not to smoke or drink or do drugs. Do not be homosexual, get tattoos, or hang around with those who do (sorry, I had to).

I'm not making light of sin, but those are not the commandments that John was talking about in this passage. John talks about Jesus' specific command in John 13:34, which is repeated in John 15:12: *"love one another as I have loved you."*

We can see that by what John says next in 1 John 2.

1 John 2:8-11
On the other hand, I am writing a new commandment to you, which is true in Him and in you, because the darkness is passing away and the true Light is already shining. The one who says that he is in the Light and yet hates his brother or sister is in the darkness until now. The one who loves his brother and sister remains in the Light, and there is nothing in him to cause stumbling. But the one who hates his brother or sister is in the darkness and walks in the darkness, and does not know where he is going because the darkness has blinded his eyes.

So, as you can see, John was not referring to Moses'

commandments but Jesus' "new commandment" to love one another. This command from Jesus trumps all of the previous commandments. Paul said this plainly in Galatians 5:14, *"the entire law is fulfilled in keeping this one command: "Love your neighbor as yourself."*

WHAT DOES IT MEAN TO HATE?

What I find most fascinating about 1 John 2 is John's usage of the word hate. Twice, he said, *"hates his brother or sister,"* meaning the opposite of love. Well, that makes sense, right? And yet, our English translation of hate is so weak. It is easy to dismiss that John could be talking about me in this verse because, while I don't like some people, I certainly don't hate them. Right?

The Greek word for hate that John used here is μισέω or *miseó* which directly translated means "detest, love less, and esteem less." Wait, love less and esteem less? Less than what? Well, less than myself for starters.

Ouch. It gets worse.

This word can also be translated to mean "to postpone in love or esteem, to slight, through oversight of the circumstance, or disregard and indifference to a thing."[1]

So, John says that when we are indifferent to our brothers or sisters or disregard their needs, we are hating, which renders us back into darkness.

That is serious.

Sin is not just breaking a rule; it's also neglecting, disregarding or acting with indifference. That's why when Jesus referred to the law, He said, *"You have heard it said…but I say."* His love is next level.

Religion gets preoccupied with the don'ts, in ourselves and in others, to such a degree that we neglect what we *should* do. We get so focused on sinners and their sins that we disregard their needs. We get so wrapped up in being right that we aren't able to be "one."

Do you see the Pharisee in the mirror? When I look in the

mirror, I see one.

Religion preoccupies man until he finds the Kingdom. The church has been at its best when it focuses more on *doing* the work of the ministry than on *being* right. Christianity is irresistible when it stands for a who, instead of propagating a view, and when it acts in love and doesn't disregard the needs among us. History tells us that some of the church's brightest moments came when the world was in its darkest moments.

The lampstand was in place, and it was beautiful.

WHEN WE GET IT RIGHT

The church experienced its most explosive growth between 200-300 AD. Christianity entered the third century with an estimated congregation of just under 218,000 members. By the end of the century, the church is said to have been just over 6,000,000 with an estimated 43% growth rate per decade.[2]

That's incredible!

What was the cause of this explosion in growth? What made the church so irresistible in a time that also records some of the greatest persecution against the church?

In 249, a deadly plague swept across the Roman empire. The Cyprian Plague lasted until 262 and was estimated to have wiped out about a fifth of the population of the entire empire.

Pontius of Carthage wrote of the plague, saying:

> Afterwards there broke out a dreadful plague, and excessive destruction of a hateful disease invaded every house in succession of the trembling populace, carrying off day by day with abrupt attack numberless people, every one from his own house. All were shuddering, fleeing, shunning the contagion, impiously exposing their own friends, as if with the exclusion of the person who was sure to die of the plague, one could

> exclude death itself also. There lay about the meanwhile, over the whole city, no longer bodies, but the carcasses of many, and, by the contemplation of a lot which in their turn would be theirs, demanded the pity of the passers-by for themselves. No one regarded anything besides his cruel gains. No one trembled at the remembrance of a similar event. No one did to another what he himself wished to experience.[3]

While everyone in the empire reacted with fear and retreated from the sick and dying, even fleeing from their own families and friends, Christians responded differently.

Dionysius, bishop of Alexandria, wrote:

> Most of our brethren, through their surpassing love and brotherly kindness being unsparing of themselves and clinging to one another, fearlessly visiting the sick and continually ministering to them, serving them in Christ, most cheerfully departed this life with them, becoming infected with the affliction of others and drawing the sickness from their neighbors upon themselves and willingly taking over their pains.[4]

Christians were blamed for the plague. The Romans believed that the plague was 'the punishment of the gods' because Roman citizens were abandoning their worship of them. This paranoia led to some of the harshest persecutions against the church ever.

There was the Decian persecution of the early 250s, followed immediately by the persecutions under Emperor Valerian, which led to the harshest of all, the Diocletian persecution from 283-305 AD.

Yet, despite the horrors of the plague and the subsequent persecution, the church exploded in numbers. Why? Because the church was a bright light in a dark time. Because Christians remained focused on their mission, even to their own peril, and ministered to the "least of these." They refused to be distracted. They refused to be indifferent. They refused to put their needs above those of the people around them, even when those around them were persecuting and killing them.

Dr. Myles Monroe said it best when he said,

> The Kingdom of which we are a part is so powerful that we need not fear any potential opposition. Kingdom men and women say, "Bring on the problems," and we will advance right through them. Our Kingdom does not run and it does not retreat; our King stands firm, advances, and overcomes.[5]

The Cyprian Plague was named after Bishop Cyprian of Carthage because he was an early Christian writer who witnessed and described the plague.[6] Inspired by Bishop Cyprian and the church's response to the plague a century before, Bishop Basil and his church in Caesarea responded similarly to the devastating drought and subsequent famine in 368-369.

Bishop Basil was quoted as saying,

> The bread you store belongs to the hungry. The clothes you accumulate belong to the naked. The shoes that you have in your closet are for the barefoot. The money you bury deep into the ground to keep it safe, belongs to the poor. You were unfair to as many people as you could have helped and you did not.[7]

Again, Christians didn't run from problems. They ran toward them. They didn't abdicate responsibilities. They accepted them instead and offered efficient solutions. Their work was so effective that a city had to be built outside of Caesarea just to house them all. In that city, called Basilica, was the world's very first hospital, a complete nursing center under one roof that became the inspiration for our modern hospitals today.

Medical historian Geunter B. Risse, in his book *Mending Bodies, Saving Souls: A History of Hospitals*, said in regard to the early church:

> Joining this religion, the Christians, ensured membership in a dedicated network of believers, whose family values protected orphans and widows, and whose nursing services were eagerly sought.[8]

CARE FOR THE SICK

Bishop Basil and Bishop Cyprian have not been the only Christians who have responded to the need for health care. By the beginning of the 5th century, inspired by Basil, the hospital had already become ubiquitous throughout the Christian East in the Byzantine world, a dramatic shift from the pre-Christian era of the Roman Empire, where no civilian hospitals existed. These medical facilities resembled a city and included housing for doctors and nurses and separate buildings for various classes of patients. There was a separate section for lepers. Some hospitals maintained libraries and training programs; doctors compiled their medical and pharmacological studies in manuscripts. Thus, in-patient medical care, in the sense of what we today consider a hospital, was an invention "driven by Christian mercy and Byzantine innovation."[9]

John Dickerson said in his book *Jesus Skeptic*, "As compassionate as the earliest Christian hospitals were, it was the knowledge gained during the Scientific Revolution (also launched by Christians) and in the universities (also started by Christians) that moved Christian hospitals from mere centers of compassion to places of scientific learning and advancement."[10]

One of those advancements came from another Christian who was responding to the needs around him. His name was

Edward Jenner (1749-1823). Jenner is often called "the father of immunology," and his work is said to have "saved more lives than the work of any other human."[11] Jenner invented the vaccine in response to smallpox, which was a leading cause of death in 18th Century Europe, killing an estimated 400,000 Europeans each year.[12]

Jenner said, "I am not surprised that men are not grateful to me, but I wonder that they are not grateful to God for the good which he has made me the instrument of conveying to my fellow creatures."[13]

Another great Christian contributor to health care was Florence Nightingale (1820-1910). On October 21, 1854, she and the staff of 38 volunteer nurses were sent to the front of the Crimean War. Nightingale arrived at Selimiye Barracks in Scutari early in November 1854. Her team found that poor care for wounded soldiers was being delivered by overworked medical staff in the face of official indifference. Medicines were in short supply, hygiene was being neglected, and mass infections were common, many of them fatal. There was no equipment to process food for the patients.[14]

Nightingale responded to the horrific conditions by sending a plea to *The Times* newspaper in London asking for a government solution. The British government responded and commissioned Isambard Kingdom Brunel to design a prefabricated hospital that could be built in England and shipped to the Dardanelles. The result was Renkioi Hospital, a civilian facility that, under the management of Edmund Alexander Parkes, had a death rate less than one-tenth of that of Scutari.

In the *Dictionary of National Biography*, Stephen Paget asserted that Nightingale reduced the death rate from 42% to 2% by improving hygiene herself or calling for the Sanitary Commission. For example, Nightingale implemented handwashing and other hygiene practices in the war hospital where she worked. She is known as the founder of modern nursing.[15]

What motivated Nightingale? She said, "Christ, indeed, came

into the world to save sinners, to wash them with his blood, to deliver men from sin and its consequences, to establish the kingdom of heaven with him."[16]

She was motivated by the King and His Kingdom to eliminate not just sin but the "consequences" of sin. For her, that meant ministering to the sick and wounded.

Did you know that our modern hospital system in North America was driven by the church? In the 1800s, there were no hospitals as we have today. Doctors were only available for house calls, which was often very expensive, meaning the poor frequently had to go without care. Christian pastors and leaders, seeing the need and not wanting to disregard the "least of these" or act indifferent to the needs around them, began casting the vision for medical facilities that would gather doctors in one place and provide care for everyone, not just the rich. Soon, Christian donors stepped up and began funding this dream. Christian universities offered to supply trained doctors and nurses, and hospitals were built and staffed around the continent.[17]

Another excellent example of the church responding to a need happened in the late 1800s. On August 21, 1883, a tornado struck Rochester, killing at least 37 people and injuring over 200 more.[18] One-third of the town was destroyed. Following the tornado, Mother Alfred Moes saw the need for a hospital in the town. She proposed to Dr. William Worrall Mayo that the Sisters would operate a hospital for the injured and sick if he and his sons would serve as its physicians. Thus, they opened St. Mary's Hospital on September 30, 1889. Today, that hospital is a part of the famous Mayo Clinic, one of the top 15 medical centers in the world.[19]

John S. Dickerson said, "Ten out of ten of the top hospitals in the United States began with medical doctors who were trained by Christian universities, and nine out of ten had Christian founders who declared their Christian faith as their motive for establishing the hospital."[20]

EDUCATION

Christians haven't just responded to health needs. The church has also been the leading force behind our modern education systems. Right from the onset, the church began to build schools.

The first schools were known as Catechetical schools. The first record of these schools came from Christian historian Jerome (347-420), who claimed the Alexandrian school was founded by John Mark the Apostle (author of the Gospel of Mark) in the second century. The chronicled dean, said to be appointed by Mark, was Justus of Alexandria, who was the school's overseer from 62-118 AD and died in 129 AD.[21]

The Catechetical schools gave birth to the Monastic schools after the time of Constantine. The Monastic schools, as you can probably tell by the name, mainly were intended for monks and nuns who were required to actively engage in reading. This reading took on the characteristics of a school that dealt with both religious and secular subjects.

Beginning in the fifth century, various leaders of the monasteries took upon themselves the responsibility of educating those who entered the monastery at a young age. The earliest of these monastic schools had more of a spiritual and ascetic focus than a scriptural or theological one, but it has been suggested that these were the qualities that led many monks trained at the monastic schools to be selected as bishops.[22]

In the sixth century, these Monastic schools gave birth to Cathedral schools. Some Cathedral schools from the sixth century remain in existence today, including the King's School, Canterbury (founded in 597, the King's School, Rochester (founded in 604), and St.Peter's School, York (founded in 627).

The Cathedral schools formed the spine of K-12 education

and introduced post-secondary education. Around 1000 AD, the Cathedral schools introduced further education called the "universita," Latin for "the whole, total, or universe." You guessed it, today's modern university. Oxford was the first University birthed from a Cathedral school and is on record as having started in 1096.[23]

Christian education was responsible for the Scientific Revolution of 1543-1687. Sociologist Rodney Stark explored the journals and personal artifacts of the fifty-two most influential scientists who launched the scientific revolution. He found that 98% of the founders were committed Christians, including Isaac Newton, Johannes Kepler, Blaise Pascal, Robert Boyle, John Ray, and more.[24] In fact, Isaac Newton wrote more than four million words of theology.[25] That's the equivalent of 63 books.

The fact that Christianity had such a massive influence on science debunks the modern claim that science disproves the Christian faith. The education provided in the church schools led to the Scientific Revolution. We have science as we know it now because of the church.

I don't think that there is any coincidence that the Scientific Revolution began only twenty-six years after the Protestant Reformation led by Martin Luther. One of the main things Luther was adamant about is that Christians should start reading the Bible for themselves. According to Newton, the Bible and the understanding of God's Kingdom provided the foundation necessary to unlock the secrets of science.

Newton penned these words,

> This most beautiful system of the sun, planets, and comets could only proceed from the counsel and dominion of an intelligent and powerful being. This being governs all things, not as the soul of the world, but as the Lord over all, and on account of his dominion, he is wont to be called "Lord, God."[26]

The sixteenth century brought many significant contributions from the church to the world. Not only did it provide the Protestant Reformation and the Scientific Revolution, but Martin Luther and his friend, Philip Melanchthon, established the first equivalent of public education, which provided a way for tax-funded schooling for all children.

Educational reform was urgent at the beginning of the sixteenth century. At that time, no school system existed, and teaching was often limited to the children of wealthy merchants and city rulers. Luther was at the forefront of those who realized the need for change in education, and with characteristic zeal, he sought to provide education to all children in Wittenberg and throughout Germany.[27]

Another Protestant reformer in the sixteenth century was Johannes Sturm, who introduced the "graded" system into education. His ideal in education was "to direct the aspiration of the scholars toward God, to develop their intelligence, and to render them useful citizens by teaching them the skill to communicate their thoughts and sentiments with persuasive effect."[28]

These reforms greatly influenced the Western education system. In 1647, American Christians introduced a law called the "Ye Ole Deluder Satan Act." It required that any village with more than fifty households start a school and teach their children how to read.[29]

I love the name of this law. It makes me laugh. It was called this because Christians sought to create a literate population to ensure that, as the law put it, "ye old deluder, Satan" could not use illiteracy to "keep men from the knowledge of ye Scriptures."[30]

This was the same motivation that birthed colleges and universities across North America. In fact, 167 of the first 182 colleges and universities in the United States and Canada were started by Christians with the express purpose of teaching people to read the Bible.[31] These include Harvard, Yale, Princeton, Stanford and more.

ABDICATION

It's too bad that these schools and other universities today contradict their roots. There is a universal rise in anti-Christian rhetoric across higher education today.[32]

Is this the world's fault or our fault?

Most Christians want to blame the world. We call out the universities, the politicians, and businesses for not holding to Christian values. But hold on a minute. Why are we surprised when the lost act lost?

Jesus called us the "light of the world." Darkness has no power in and of itself. It is simply the absence of light. Complaining about the darkness or expecting it just not to be as dark won't make it go away. What makes darkness disappear is light.

According to the Apostle John, *"the one who hates his brother or sister is in the darkness and walks in the darkness, and does not know where he is going because the darkness has blinded his eyes."*[33]

The word that got translated into English as hate does not mean to despise; it means to disregard or show indifference. In other words, we hate if we simply ignore our brother or sister in need. If we show indifference to the needs around us, we are in the darkness. Indifference is what causes us to lose our light.

To disregard or become indifferent to something or someone means to abdicate. The word abdicate in the American dictionary means "to give up a position as king, or to fail to take responsibility for something." That is precisely what we do when we abdicate our Christian responsibilities. We are called to be ambassadors in this world for the King. We were created to rule. We were made on purpose, for a purpose, for such a time as this. When we disregard or become indifferent to the needs of others, relinquishing our authority as little-k-kings is a foregone conclusion,

Christianity prospers when Christians behave as kings and take problems 'head on.' The light shines brightest when we obey the command of our King, loving as He loved, serving the "least of these," bringing His Kingdom to earth.

Religion seeks to take the world to heaven. The Kingdom seeks to bring heaven to the world. Jesus taught us to pray, "Your kingdom come." Religion wants to escape the world and its problems. The Kingdom impacts, influences and changes the world. Religion reaches up to God. The Kingdom is God coming down to man. Religion focuses on heaven. The Kingdom focuses on the earth. Religion prepares man to leave Earth. The Kingdom empowers man to dominate Earth.[34]

When I say the word dominate, I'm not referring to lording over. I am speaking of our God-given right to rule and to have dominion. Jesus taught us to take dominion by becoming the servant of all. Every world-changing Christian I mentioned in this chapter became great, recorded in the history books because they led by serving the needs around them. They saw a problem and addressed it with excellence. They saw darkness and became the light. They didn't just pray for a solution, but they became the solution.

A modern-day example of this is Mother Teresa. She became one of the greatest influencers on the planet, not by using wealth or power, but by being a servant to the "least of these." Kings and kingdoms would listen to her and heed her counsel because she modeled Christ and carried His authority.

LET'S TAKE OUR JOB BACK

Our challenge today is to take our job back. We don't have to look very far to see problems. Darkness is all around us. We can sit around and wait for our rescue, or we can become the light in the darkness.

The COVID pandemic revealed to us and the world that our current healthcare system is flawed. Christians took responsibility at one time to create a healthcare system that worked with such excellence that the world, Christian or not, copied the system because it worked. What if we stepped back in and took our job back?

Most of us will agree that our current education system is archaic and broken. Christians once took responsibility by creating and recreating the system with such excellence that the world followed suit. What if we did it again and took our job back?

Christianity, in its original form, is not so heavenly-minded that it is no earthly good. The Kingdom is more than a belief system. Believers don't change the world. Doers do. Christianity isn't expressed best from a pulpit. It is expressed best on the street; meeting needs and ministering to the "least of these."

Let's not reduce our Christianity to a weekly gathering and disregard the problem our co-worker is having at work or become dismissive of the struggling family down the street. We don't stop being Christians when the Sunday service is over. That's where it should begin.

CHAPTER TWELVE
THE SOCIAL GOSPEL

To abdicate is to hate. To abdicate our God-given responsibility is to give up our position as stewards of our territory, the earth.

Nehemiah refused to abdicate. Instead, he accepted responsibility and dared to believe that God could use him, even though he was a prisoner of war and just a cupbearer. He understood who his King was. He understood who he was as a citizen of that kingdom. He understood the government and the laws and statutes of his King. He understood the territory of Jerusalem was the promised land and, therefore, was rightfully theirs. This understanding of the Kingdom of God gave Nehemiah the courage to move ahead and rebuild a city.

God created the heavens and the earth. That means that the earth is part of His Kingdom. His Kingdom is not just in heaven, but it is here, too. He created man to rule and have dominion over this colony.

When Adam sinned, he didn't lose a religion. He lost a territory. Jesus came to take it back. When Jesus ascended into heaven, He proclaimed that He had all of the authority back, and then He commissioned His followers once again to expand His Kingdom on earth.

Paul called us ambassadors and rulers with the authority to represent the King in this part of the Kingdom. We were created to rule, but our King commanded us to rule with His kind of love, selfless, sacrificial, and with a servant's heart. We were never commissioned to build a religion or personal castles. We were commissioned to create a movement, an assembly with a purpose to represent our King to the "least of these." Anything less than that purpose would be moving our lampstand, burying our light under a basket, and living in darkness.

The church has best shone that light when it fed the hungry during famines, cared for and cured the sick during plagues, and tackled poverty and ignorance by creating educational systems every child could receive regardless of income. The church has done much more than that, of course. I don't think it's a coincidence that some of the greatest revivals in history occurred when the greatest needs of society were met by the greatest activity of the church.

Teresa Morgan, Professor of Graeco-Roman History at the University of Oxford, said in 2019 in an interview with John Dickson,

> Christians are taught that God loves them absolutely and that on that basis they can trust God, they can love God, and, because they are given such an abundance of love, they can afford to love one another with enormous, unreserved generosity. That is a completely different model of relations with your fellow human beings, and how your relationship with God affects your relationship with human beings, from anything in ancient religious thinking in general, apart from Judaism. It is certainly completely different from anything that is in popular moral consciousness. And with that idea of love goes care of the vulnerable. This is a world with no social

> safety nets. But Christians create social safety nets. They are the people who are notorious for looking after the widows, the poor, the orphans, the people who in most of society are just slung out onto the street.[1]

Where are those safety nets today? I fear that we have entered a time in history where we have abdicated much of our responsibilities back to society and have reduced Christianity to a weekly social gathering and a private, personal belief system. Furthermore, our belief system is clearer about what it stands against than what it stands for.

I know many Christians and churches are not to be lumped in with this generalization, but I'm not addressing them. I'm talking to the rest of us. I'm also speaking from a bird's eye view of the global church. How is it that many outsiders classify modern-day followers of Jesus as racist bigots who follow an antiquated system of beliefs irrelevant to life today? How has Christianity become so resistible to a world that needs hope more than ever?

Abdicated responsibilities.

The church used to run the education system, but slowly, over time, we abdicated and allowed secular governments and agencies to take over.

The church used to run the entire healthcare system. That's why a majority of hospitals, still to this day, have a Christian name. In recent history, we have abdicated this responsibility and allowed governments and secular organizations to take over. Today, only one in five patients in the US receive treatment from a "religious hospital."[2] In Canada, the vast majority of hospitals and medical centers are run by the government because of universal healthcare.

SOCIAL JUSTICE

At one time, the church was the most active participant in

social services and social justice. For example, Christians have been responsible for defending women's rights throughout history. Roman authorities said that Christians were difficult to identify in the first three centuries because they dressed and acted the same as every other Roman citizen. However, there was one identifiable difference. Christian men would treat their wives and daughters with honor and respect. In Roman society, women were considered inferior. But, Christian men would treat women as equals and would be seen in public walking with their wives and daughters, something a Roman man would never be caught doing.

In the 16th century, the Reformation in Europe allowed more women to add their voices, including the English writers Jane Anger, Aemilia Lanyer, and the prophetess Anna Trapnell. English and American Quakers (Protestant Christian denomination) believed that men and women were equal. Many Quaker women were preachers.[3]

Besides fighting for the equality of women, Christians like William Wilberforce and others fought for the abolishment of slavery. Wilberforce was a Kingdom thinker. He dedicated his entire life to ridding slavery in England. Not all Christians stood with him. Yet, he persisted. He is quoted as saying, "What a difference it would be if our system of morality were based on the Bible instead of the standards devised by cultural Christians."[4]

It's ironic that a Christian could ever be labeled as a racist. Although, in some cases, the label is warranted, the most significant battles fought against systemic racism were led by Christians. The Reverend Martin Luther King is a prime example. King said, "If one is truly devoted to the religion of Jesus, he will seek to rid the earth of social evils. The gospel is social as well as personal."[5]

I love that. The gospel is social as well as personal. Yes, it is. James, the brother of Jesus, said virtually the same thing in James 2.

James 2:14-26
What good is it, my brothers and sisters, if someone claims to have faith but has no deeds? Can such faith save them? Suppose a brother or a sister is without clothes and daily food. If one of you says to them, "Go in peace; keep warm and well fed," but does nothing about their physical needs, what good is it? In the same way, faith by itself, if it is not accompanied by action, is dead. But someone will say, "You have faith; I have deeds." Show me your faith without deeds, and I will show you my faith by my deeds. You believe that there is one God. Good! Even the demons believe that—and shudder. You foolish person, do you want evidence that faith without deeds is useless? Was not our father Abraham considered righteous for what he did when he offered his son Isaac on the altar? You see that his faith and his actions were working together, and his faith was made complete by what he did. And the scripture was fulfilled that says, "Abraham believed God, and it was credited to him as righteousness," and he was called God's friend. You see that a person is considered righteous by what they do and not by faith alone. In the same way, was not even Rahab the prostitute considered righteous for what she did when she gave lodging to the spies and sent them off in a different direction? As the body without the spirit is dead, so faith without deeds is dead.

James said that a personal faith without public deeds is dead. It is nothing. It doesn't matter how much a person can quote chapter and verse or how Christian they say they are. What matters is how they prove their faith by their actions.

What actions? According to James, Isaiah, and Jesus, physical and emotional needs must be met as much or more than spiritual needs.

While I can somewhat understand why the church abdicated its responsibility in healthcare and education (it is costly), I cannot grasp how we have also abdicated much of the social gospel.

Today, there are more than 1.5 million charities in the United States.[6] Only 345,000 of those are churches.[7] In Canada, there are 85,000 charitable organizations[8] and 30,000 churches.[9]

Pew Research Center investigators examined the behavior of a large sample of the public across a typical seven-day period. They found that among Americans who attend services weekly and pray daily, 45 percent had done volunteer work during the previous week. Among all other Americans, only 27 percent had volunteered somewhere. A 2013 report found that 73 percent of all charitable giving in the U.S. goes to explicitly religious organizations. Other research shows that of America's top 50 charities, 40 percent are faith-based.[10] If these reports are accurate, why is the church not more widely known for leading the way in meeting the greatest needs in society?

THE BIRTH OF THE SOCIAL GOSPEL

In the late 19th century, many Christians in the US were disgusted by the poverty level and the low quality of living in the slums. In 1879, Pastor Charles Oliver Brown and journalist Henry George wrote a book entitled *Progress and Poverty*. The book coined the term "the social gospel" and created a movement under the same name.

The Social Gospel became a social movement within Protestantism that aimed to apply Christian ethics to social problems, especially issues of social justice such as economic inequality, poverty, alcoholism, crime, racial tensions, slums, unclean environment, child labor, lack of unionization, poor schools, and the dangers of war. It was most prominent in the early-20th-century United States and Canada.[11]

The Social Gospel affected much of Protestant America. The Presbyterians described their goals in 1910 by proclaiming:

> The great ends of the church are the proclamation of the gospel for the salvation of humankind; the shelter, nurture, and spiritual fellowship of the children of God; the maintenance of divine worship; the preservation of truth; the promotion of social righteousness; and the exhibition of the Kingdom of Heaven to the world.[12]

Great vision.

On top of that, the Social Gospelers made it their focus to put into practice the Lord's Prayer, specifically, "*Thy kingdom come, Thy will be done on earth as it is in heaven.*"[13]

Another of the defining theologians for the Social Gospel movement was Walter Rauschenbusch, a Baptist pastor of the Second German Baptist Church in Hell's Kitchen, New York. In 1907, he published a book entitled *Christianity and the Social Crisis*, which would influence the actions of several actors of the social gospel. In 1917, Rauschenbusch wrote another influential book *A Theology for the Social Gospel.* He claimed that "the individualistic gospel has made sinfulness of the individual clear, but it has not shed light on institutionalized sinfulness."This ideology would be inherited by liberation theologians, civil rights advocates, and leaders such as Martin Luther King Jr.[14]

To be honest, until doing the research needed for this book, I had never heard of the Social Gospel or the books *Progress and Poverty, Christianity and the Social Crisis*, or *A Theology for the Social Gospel.* While I have not read these books, what I have read of their ideologies and initial reasoning sounded eerily similar to the arguments I have made in this book. However, much to my surprise, I discovered that the leaders of the Social Gospel movement mainly were theologically liberal, although a few were also conservative. Rauschenbusch, for instance, railed against what he regarded as the "selfishness of capitalism" and promoted instead a form of Christian socialism that supported the creation of labor unions and cooperative economics.[15]

While the movement itself is said to have died off immediately following the First World War, the impacts of the Social Gospel have been long-lasting. Biographer Randall Woods argued that the Social Gospel themes learned from childhood allowed President Lyndon B. Johnson to transform social problems into moral problems. This helps explain his longtime commitment to social justice, exemplified by *the Great Society* and his commitment to racial equality. The Social Gospel explicitly inspired his foreign-policy approach to a sort of Christian internationalism and nation-building.[16]

The Social Gospel, after 1945, influenced the formation of Christian democracy and political ideology among Protestants and Catholics in Europe. In Canada, it influenced the *Cooperative Commonwealth Federation*, a political party that was later reformulated as the *New Democratic Party*. The CCF was founded on social gospel principles in the 1930s by J. S. Woodsworth, a Methodist minister, and Alberta MP William Irvine. Woodsworth wrote extensively about the Social Gospel from experiences gained while working with immigrant slum dwellers in Winnipeg from 1904 to 1913. His writings called for the Kingdom of God "here and now." This political party took power in the province of Saskatchewan in 1944, led by Tommy Douglas, a Baptist minister, who introduced universal medicare, family allowance and old age pensions. This political party has since essentially lost its religious basis and became a secular social democratic party.[17]

How does a movement started on the same principles we have covered so far (caring for the "least of these" with an emphasis on the Kingdom of God) turn into liberal socialism?

HOW THE SOCIAL GOSPEL BECOMES SOCIALISM

It happens in the same way that Emperor Julian the Apostate

stole the best practices of the Christians he hated and made them his own. He had observed Christians closely and had concluded that it was the fact that they "devoted themselves to philanthropy" that "they have led very many into atheism."[18] (He called Christians atheists because they did not worship the Roman gods).

He said in a letter to Arsacius, the pagan high priest of Galatia,

> I have but now made a plan by which you may be well provided for this; for I have given directions that 30,000 modii (59,400 dry gallons, weighing more than 2 tons) of corn shall be assigned every year for the whole of Galatia, and 60,000 pints (28,000 liters) of wine. I order that one-fifth of this be used for the poor who serve priests, and the remainder be distributed by us to strangers and beggars. For it is disgraceful that, when no Jew ever has to beg, and the impious Galileans (another term he used for Christians meant to degrade them) support not only their own poor but ours as well, all men see that our people lack aid from us. [19]

From the beginning of time, people have taken the principles of the scriptures and used them for their own gain. Why? Because they work regardless of who uses them. They are like the law of gravity. God created it, yet it works the same for believers and unbelievers. I believe the reason the Social Gospel movement could become a socialist political movement is because the principles and practices proved fruitful and because Christians stepped away from their posts and abdicated their responsibilities.

When we, as Christians, withdraw from influential posts in society and reduce our faith to a weekly gathering, we withdraw the light with us. The light of Christianity is not meant to be kept under a basket. It is not meant to only shine in a temple on a given day of the week. The gospel of the Kingdom is meant to transform all seven pillars of society—business, government, education, family, media, entertainment, and religion. When we reduce our governing influence to just one of the seven pillars, employ religious tendencies, and minimize our faith to a private vertical relationship with God, we lack an understanding of the Kingdom of God and our King.

> 1 John 3:11, 16-18
> *For this is the message you heard from the beginning: We should love one another.*
>
> *This is how we know what love is: Jesus Christ laid down his life for us. And we ought to lay down our lives for our brothers and sisters. If anyone has material possessions and sees a brother or sister in need but has no pity on them, how can the love of God be in that person? Dear children, let us not love with words or speech but with actions and in truth.*

Our relationship with God demands more of us than mere words. It requires more than personal and private disciplines. It asks more of us than just attending a building with other believers once a week. It's more than accumulating knowledge. It requires obedience.

> 1 John 3:23
> *And this is his command: to believe in the name of his Son, Jesus Christ, and to love one another as he commanded us.*

To believe Jesus is Lord is a personal decision. To act like He is Lord requires a public response. If we have *"material possessions and see a brother or sister in need,"* we should do more than just pray for them. We should do all we can to meet their needs.

HAVE WE ABDICATED GRACE?

Do you know why people are drawn to socialism, critical theory, critical race theory, and the LGBTQ2+ community? Because that is where they feel the most loved and accepted. People are naturally drawn to where they feel acceptance, a sense of belonging, and identity. Unfortunately, we have abdicated that as well.

Some groups in our society are more tolerant, loving, and gracious to sinners than the "Christ-like-ones." This shouldn't be. Jesus was the greatest example of love and acceptance. He loved and accepted people who were nothing like Him, and those who were nothing like Him loved and accepted Him back! Whether it was the outcast tax collectors like Matthew and Zaccheus, prostitutes, women caught in adultery, lepers banished from their community, lowly Samaritans, or the Roman Centurion. It didn't matter to Jesus what someone did or why they were considered unlovable. Jesus loved and accepted them all. And then he said, *"Go and do likewise."* [20] *"Love like I have loved you."*[21]

Our mission as Christians ought to be to out-love, out-serve, and out-give everyone, everywhere, every time.

How do we outlove?

> 1 Corinthians 13:1-3
>
> *If I speak in the tongues of men or of angels, but do not have love, I am only a resounding gong or a clanging cymbal. If I have the gift of prophecy and can fathom all mysteries and all knowledge, and if I have a faith that can move mountains, but do not have love, I am nothing. If I give all I possess to the poor and give over my body to hardship that I may boast, but do not have love, I gain nothing.*

I recently spoke with a pastor who told me that someone on his board asked him, "Why should we change how we do church for unsaved people? Why should I have to 'suffer' to make it more comfortable for them?"

Did you hear the gong?

We aren't loving with the love of Christ when we make our faith and worship all about us. We must love others more than ourselves. This is a challenge to out-love everyone, everywhere, every time.

You might be thinking, but hold on, we can't get competitive with this thing. What do you mean by outlove? Paul told us to be competitive with our love and honor in Romans 12.

> Romans 12:10 (ESV)
> *Love one another with brotherly affection. Outdo one another in showing honor.*

Paul gave us insight on how we can outlove the world. He broke down the Jesus-kind of love into bite-sized pieces.

> 1 Corinthians 13:4-8, 13
> *Love is patient, love is kind. It does not envy, it does not boast, it is not proud. It does not dishonor others, it is not self-seeking, it is not easily angered, it keeps no record of wrongs. Love does not delight in evil but rejoices with the truth. It always protects, always trusts, always hopes, always perseveres. Love never fails. And now these three remain: faith, hope and love. But the greatest of these is love.*

Patience means to move at the pace of another. It means that we won't run ahead of someone. It also means we won't drag someone down and insist they join our pace. Kindness means to lend someone your strength rather than reminding them of their weakness. Honor means to defer to others, valuing them over yourself. We become self-seeking when we value our own reputation over someone else's needs.

Easily angered simply means easily stirred up. No one can make us angry. To respond in anger is a choice we make ourselves.

Keeping no record of wrongs means that we forgive and seek the restoration of the relationship. Not delighting in evil means we aren't waiting for someone to do wrong; we expect them to do right. Love protects when it protects others above its own reputation.

Love always trusts. Always is a huge word.

Nothing on this list is easy to do. This kind of love is very uncommon. But let's think about it for a moment. We all want to be loved in this way. We want others to be patient with us. We want others to be kind and selfless. We are grateful when others don't hold grudges. You get the point.

Paul finishes the chapter with the statement that the "greatest of these is love." He's not kidding. This kind of love is a game-changer.

Imagine loving like this at work tomorrow. Imagine loving your neighbors like this. Imagine loving your family (yes, even the irritating ones) like this. Imagine extending this kind of love to everyone you meet, everywhere, all the time. You would become the most popular person in your community. Irresistible.

OUTLOVE, OUTSERVE, OUTGIVE

Now, what if we also accepted the challenge to out-serve everyone, everywhere, at every time? Jesus tried to drill this into his disciples multiple times.

> Matthew 23:1-12
> *Then Jesus said to the crowds and to his disciples: "The teachers of the law and the Pharisees sit in Moses' seat. So you must be careful to do everything they tell you. But do not do what they do, for they do not practice what they preach. They tie up heavy, cumbersome loads and put them on other people's shoulders, but they themselves are not willing to lift a finger to move them.*

"Everything they do is done for people to see: They make their phylacteries wide and the tassels on their garments long; they love the place of honor at banquets and the most important seats in the synagogues; they love to be greeted with respect in the marketplaces and to be called 'Rabbi' by others. "But you are not to be called 'Rabbi,' for you have one Teacher, and you are all brothers. And do not call anyone on earth 'father,' for you have one Father, and he is in heaven. Nor are you to be called instructors, for you have one Instructor, the Messiah. The greatest among you will be your servant. For those who exalt themselves will be humbled, and those who humble themselves will be exalted.

Jesus was calling out the religious. The Pharisees believed in God. They feared God and obeyed the rules set out by Moses. Yet, in their focus on getting it right, they got it wrong. Imagine, they had dedicated their entire lives to getting to know God and living with great anticipation for the Messiah to show up, yet there He was, in person, in their generation, and they missed Him.

They were so focused on building their own kingdoms that they missed *the* Kingdom. How do we avoid doing the same? Surprisingly, the answer isn't getting closer to God. According to Jesus, the answer is actually in serving others with humility.

Mark 10:42-45
Jesus called them together and said, "You know that those who are regarded as rulers of the Gentiles lord it over them, and their high officials exercise authority over them. Not so with you. Instead, whoever wants to become great among you must be your servant, and whoever wants to be first must be slave of all. For even the Son of Man did not come to be served, but to serve, and to give his life as a ransom for many."

The world's kingdoms are built on command and control hierarchies. God's Kingdom is built on love and servitude. The greatest in God's Kingdom are those who out-serve everyone else. The early church proved this. They out-served the greatest empire on the planet, and the most powerful ruler at the time envied them and sought to copy their tactics.

How do we take our job back? We out-love, we out-serve, and we out-give.

Jesus taught his disciples an invaluable lesson in his interaction with a rich, young ruler.

> Mark 10:17-23
> *As Jesus started on his way, a man ran up to him and fell on his knees before him. "Good teacher," he asked, "what must I do to inherit eternal life?" "Why do you call me good?" Jesus answered. "No one is good—except God alone. You know the commandments: 'You shall not murder, you shall not commit adultery, you shall not steal, you shall not give false testimony, you shall not defraud, honor your father and mother.'" "Teacher," he declared, "all these I have kept since I was a boy." Jesus looked at him and loved him. "One thing you lack," he said. "Go, sell everything you have and give to the poor, and you will have treasure in heaven. Then come, follow me." At this the man's face fell. He went away sad, because he had great wealth. Jesus looked around and said to his disciples, "How hard it is for the rich to enter the kingdom of God!"*

Notice that Jesus never asked for the man to give to Him. He asked the man to give to the poor. When Jesus said that He couldn't enter the Kingdom of God, He wasn't referring to this man's eternal salvation. Not giving all of His money away wasn't going to damn this man to hell.

By not giving his money to the poor, he wouldn't experience

the true government of God, which we have already learned is faith, works, and love expressed in deeds.

This was so important to the disciples that immediately after the Holy Spirit moved on them and the church was started in Acts 2, it says that *"they sold property and possessions to give to anyone who had need."*[22]

They did precisely what the rich young ruler couldn't. And yet, they didn't go without. It says in Acts 4 *"that there were no needy persons among them."* And, then again, it says, *"For from time to time those who owned land or houses sold them, brought the money from the sales and put it at the apostles' feet, and it was distributed to anyone who had need."*[23]

The church maintained this voracious generosity for at least three centuries because, as we saw in Julian the Apostate's confession, by 362 AD, the church was outgiving an empire!

The assignment of the ambassadors of the Kingdom of God is to out-love, out-serve, and out-give everyone, everywhere, at every time. Do you accept the challenge?

The next question we must answer is where. Where do we specifically focus our attention? You might be surprised to discover that the Bible is very specific as to where we go. We'll discover how specific it is in the next chapter.

CHAPTER THIRTEEN

THE CITY WITHOUT A CHURCH

In Revelation 21, the Apostle John has a vision of heaven and records it with incredible specificity. Before you look it up, I want you to envision what you imagine heaven will look like. What do you see? Hopefully, it's not a curly redhead floating on a cloud, playing a harp, spreading Philly Cream Cheese on a bagel.

No really. What do you anticipate heaven to be like?

John's vision is nothing like that. At least, how he describes heaven is nothing like what I envisioned it to be like.

I grew up in the church and have been taught much about heaven. Of course, I was taught that its streets are paved with gold and that there would be no more tears, pain, or suffering. I was happy to discover that all those things were included in John's vision of heaven. But, two things surprised me when I recently re-read John's words.

Heaven is a city. There is no Temple there.

Revelation 21:1-5
Then I saw "a new heaven and a new earth," for the first heaven and the first earth had passed away, and there was no longer any sea. I saw the Holy City, the new Jerusalem, coming down out of heaven from God, prepared as a bride beautifully dressed for her husband. And I heard a loud voice from the throne saying, "Look! God's dwelling place is now among the people, and he will dwell with them. They will be his people, and God himself will be with them and be their God. 'He will wipe every tear from their eyes. There will be no more death' or mourning or crying or pain, for the old order of things has passed away."

First of all, did you notice that God will create a new heaven and a new earth? He is going to create two locations. We cannot assume that we will spend all of eternity in heaven. The first time He created the earth, it was for us to rule and have dominion over a territory. The only reason He would create another earth is for the same purpose.

Did you also notice how proudly He will present it to us? As proud as a new bride who gets beautifully dressed to walk down the aisle to her husband. God will be so excited to present our territory—a City.

HEAVEN IS A CITY

The writer of Hebrews, multiple times, emphasized that God had in mind all along to build us a city. In speaking about Abraham in Hebrews 11:10, he said, *"For he was looking forward to the city with foundations, whose architect and builder is God."*

In speaking about the Israelites, he wrote, *"If they had been thinking of the country they had left, they would have had opportunity to return. Instead, they were longing for a better country—a heavenly one. Therefore God is not ashamed to be called their God, for he has prepared a city for them."*[1]

From the beginning, God had the ultimate goal of a city in mind. In Hebrews 13:14, the writers pressed deeper into this fact. In speaking to the early church, he writes, "*For here we do not have an enduring city, but we are looking for the city that is to come.*"

Why a city? Cities are typically dirty, corrupt, crime-ridden, and chaotic. Cities are not utopias. Yet, John, almost anticipating our reaction, describes this city as perfect.

Revelation 21:10-21

And he carried me away in the Spirit to a mountain great and high, and showed me the Holy City, Jerusalem, coming down out of heaven from God. It shone with the glory of God, and its brilliance was like that of a very precious jewel, like a jasper, clear as crystal. It had a great, high wall with twelve gates, and with twelve angels at the gates. On the gates were written the names of the twelve tribes of Israel. There were three gates on the east, three on the north, three on the south and three on the west. The wall of the city had twelve foundations, and on them were the names of the twelve apostles of the Lamb. The angel who talked with me had a measuring rod of gold to measure the city, its gates and its walls. The city was laid out like a square, as long as it was wide. He measured the city with the rod and found it to be 12,000 stadia in length, and as wide and high as it is long. The angel measured the wall using human measurement, and it was 144 cubits thick. The wall was made of jasper, and the city of pure gold, as pure as glass. The foundations of the city walls were decorated with every kind of precious stone. The first foundation was jasper, the second sapphire, the third agate, the fourth emerald, the fifth onyx, the sixth ruby, the seventh chrysolite, the eighth beryl, the ninth topaz, the tenth turquoise, the eleventh jacinth, and the twelfth amethyst. The twelve gates were twelve pearls, each gate made of a single pearl. The great street of the city was of gold, as pure as transparent glass.

John is precise in his details. I don't know about you, but when I dream, I remember the gist, but I don't remember the specifics. Therefore, we must conclude that this was definitely a vision, not a dream. God was very intentional in showing John this vision. He wanted us to have a clear understanding of what was coming.

A study from Arizona State University discovered that what people believe happens after death guides how they think about the earth and how they behave.[2] You can see this in the different behaviors demonstrated by people dependent on their religions, mainly how those behaviors are shaped by their belief in the afterlife. If that is the case, then we must assume that God gave the details of eternity because He intended it to shape our behaviors on earth as well.

This makes it more essential for us to pay attention to the specific details God gave John in the vision. First of all, God is preparing a city for us. I don't know about you, but we rarely go to cities for a vacation. We escape them. So, why a city?

Secondly, the city is beautiful. Perfect. It isn't dirty and dingy. It has a street that is pure gold. Its walls are made of jasper and pure gold. Its foundations are made of precious stones. Its gates are pearls. A single pearl (that's one giant oyster)! This sounds like a city to visit and retreat to.

Thirdly, God gave John the specific measurements of the city. It was laid out in a perfect square. According to John's measurements, the city was 1400 miles, or 2200 kilometers long, and the same distance wide. That's the same distance from where I live, Lethbridge, Alberta, Canada, to Phoenix, Arizona, USA. That's a big city!

But John also said the city was just as high. I feel sorry for those of you who are afraid of heights! Maybe God will let you live on the bottom floor.

But seriously, John said this in verse 16, *"He measured the city with the rod and found it to be 12,000 stadia in length, and as wide and high as it is long."*

Why would God get so specific? What does He want us to know?

THE DIMENSIONS OF A COMPLETE LIFE

Martin Luther King (MLK) preached a sermon on this passage on January 24, 1954, in Montgomery, Alabama, at Dexter Avenue Baptist Church. Apparently, this message was a try-out for the congregation who were considering him as their new pastor.[3]

In the message, he described why he felt it mattered that the length, width, and height of the Holy City were all equal.

> The Length of life, as we shall use it, is, of course, not its duration. It is rather the push of a life forward to its own personal ends and ambitions. It is the inward concern for achieving our own pernal end and ambitions. The Breadth of life is the outward concern for the welfare of others. The Height of life is the upward reach toward God. These are the three dimensions of life, and without the due development of all no life becomes complete.[4]

To MLK, God gave the specific dimensions of the Holy City, and in particular, the equality of the measurements, because He desired us to live life three-dimensionally, equally balancing our personal ambitions with our concern for others and our relationship with God.

What a concept. I am not certain that this is God's intended purpose, but this idea does cause me to stop and ponder living three-dimensionally.

In the sermon's other draft, King wrote the illustration further:

"At one angle stands the individual person, at the other angle stands other persons, and at the up top stands God. Unless these three are concatenated, working harmoniously together in a single life, that life is incomplete."[5]

I love how Martin Luther King does not discourage us from pursuing our own gifts and ambitions. In fact, he encourages us to do so. Many religious people, today and in times past, have discouraged people from personal pursuits to such a degree that it became a sin to pursue self-interests. This is why monasteries and nunneries became such a big deal in the past. Holiness meant completely denying self. While I commend men and women who were able to devote their lives to such a degree as to give up every self-pleasure, I also wonder if that extreme denial has led to some of the most significant controversies and abuses in church history.

The psalmist said in Psalm 139 that we were all *"beautifully and wonderfully made."*[6] We have all been given talents, gifts, and abilities from God. These giftings were given to us to solve problems and to contribute to the betterment of society. We get lopsided when we only use these talents and abilities for our personal gain.

MLK said it this way in his message:

> No man has learned to live until he can rise out of his mere concern for self to the broader concern for others. Indeed the prayer that every man should learn to pray is: "Lord teach me to unselfishly serve humanity." No man should become so involved in his personal ambitions that he forgets that other people exist in the world. Indeed if my life's work is not developed for the good of humanity, it is meaningless and Godless. Length without Breadth is dead and narrow. I say to you whatever you do in life do it for the good of humanity. Don't do it merely for the prestige that it brings or the money that it brings, but do it for the serving of humanity.[7]

In another draft of the sermon, he doubled down on this point. He commented on people who live one-dimensionally: "They brilliantly develop their inner powers, but they live as if nobody else lives in the world but themselves. Other persons become mere steps by which they climb to their personal ambitions. There is nothing more tragic than to see a person bogged down in the length of life devoid of breadth."[8]

We probably all know people like that. Hopefully, it's not us. The third dimension, according to MLK, is our relationship with God.

> The tragedy of much of modern life is that in quest of our personal and social goals we have unconsciously forgotten God. We have pursued the length and breadth of life and neglected the Height. And so we find ourselves living a disorganized, incomplete and disconnected life.[9]

I love the concept of making our lives equal in all three dimensions. I know it may sound like heresy to our pre-conditioned, religious minds to say that our relationship with God should be equal to our relationship with others and with ourselves. We would all comfortably say that our relationship with God must come first. And I agree. I believe Martin Luther King would agree, too. First, but not lopsided and to the exclusion of the other two.

We have all met people so heavenly-minded that they are no earthly good. They claim that "me and Jesus is all I need." It sounds good. But, it is lopsided and unhealthy. Even God Himself, who walked with Adam every day in the Garden of Eden, said that it is *"not good for man to be alone."*[10]

Jesus said, *"'Love the Lord your God with all your heart and with all your soul and with all your strength and with all your mind'; and, 'Love your neighbor as yourself.'"*[11]

You see, three-dimensional. Love God. Love your neighbor.

Love yourself. If you get these three out of order or unequal in their dimensions, you will become purposeless, confused, and incomplete.

NO TEMPLE THERE

The Apostle John wasn't finished with his description of the Holy City. He continued:

> Revelation 22:22-27
> *I did not see a temple in the city, because the Lord God Almighty and the Lamb are its temple. The city does not need the sun or the moon to shine on it, for the glory of God gives it light, and the Lamb is its lamp. The nations will walk by its light, and the kings of the earth will bring their splendor into it. On no day will its gates ever be shut, for there will be no night there. The glory and honor of the nations will be brought into it. Nothing impure will ever enter it, nor will anyone who does what is shameful or deceitful, but only those whose names are written in the Lamb's book of life.*

Of all of the descriptions John used for the Holy City, this might be the most shocking. The city had no temple.

It is shocking, first of all, because John was a Jew. To the Jewish people, it was ingrained in them that the temple was where God dwelled. No temple meant no presence of God. So, for John to describe the city without a temple is surprising.

Remember, how we view eternity will shape how we live on earth. Why would God expressly point out that the future city will be without a church?

Let's think about it.

If eternity were mainly spent in a temple, focusing our present life in a church would make sense. But, if our future life is to be in a Holy City without a church, then the life of those who are going there should not be focused on being *in* a church as much as *being* the church in the city.[12]

Does that mean that we should stop going to church? No, not at all, but it is a mistake to limit the focus of our faith to the worship that happens inside the four walls of a building. We aren't meant to keep our light under a basket.

Henry Drummond said it more bluntly in 1893. He wrote, "In many lands, the Churches have literally stolen Christ from the people; they have made the Son of Man the Priest of an Order; they have taken Christianity from the City and imprisoned it behind altar rails; they have withdrawn it from the national life and doled it out to the few who pay to keep up the unconscious deception."[13]

Ouch.

He wasn't done there. He preached a sermon from the pulpit of St. Mary's at Oxford University, where he doubled down on this concept.

> If it is strange that the Church of the darker ages should have needed so bitter a lesson (the actual demolition of their churches), is it not ten times stranger still that the Church of the days of greater enlightenment should be found again making the chief part of its business the organizing of the modes of worship; that the largest efforts which are owned as efforts of the Church are made for the establishment and maintenance of worship; that our chief controversies relate to the teaching and the ministry of a system designed primarily, if not exclusively, for worship: that even the fancies and refinements of such a system divide us; that the break between things secular and things religious grows wider instead of their being made to blend into one; and that the vast and fruitful spaces of the actual life of mankind lie still so largely without the gates? The old Jerusalem was all temple. The medieval

> Church was all temple. But the ideal of the new Jerusalem was—no temple, but a God-inhabited society. Are we not reversing this ideal in an age when the Church still means in so many mouths the clergy, instead of meaning the Christian society, and when nine men are striving to get men to go to church for one who is striving to make men realize that they themselves are the Church?[14]

"That our chief controversies relate to the teaching and the ministry of a system designed primarily, if not exclusively, for worship: that even the fancies and refinements of such a system divide us."

What a statement! Isn't that the truth?

THE SYSTEM DIVIDES US

Forty-five thousand denominations on the planet today. So, why does Christianity have so many branches? According to *LiveScience.com*, "A cursory look shows that differences in belief, power grabs and corruption all had a part to play."[15]

Differences in belief. The church has put all of its attention, money, and energy into being right instead of being one. We have invested everything into building castles instead of building the Kingdom of God in our cities.

I remember being told about the mansion God is preparing for me in heaven. If I put all my attention on my eternal mansion, I will focus on building castles on earth. But, if I see a Holy City without a church, I can concentrate on redeeming cities for the Kingdom of God.

> "People do not dispute that religion is in the Church. What is now wanted is to let them see it in the city. When Christianity shall take upon itself in full responsibility the burden and care

of cities the Kingdom of God will openly come to earth."[16]
~Henry Drummond

THEOLOGIES OF ESCAPISM

It's common for Christians these days to say things like, "The world is not my home" and "We're just passing through." Our focus is on escaping this big, bad, horrible world. To make matters worse, church leaders fuel this desire in us by teaching weird and wacky theologies of escapism. We were never created to "just pass through" this world. We were created to redeem it.

This is our territory. It's our responsibility.

Jeremiah 29:11 is a verse many Christians love to quote, myself included! It is often taken out of context, especially if we adhere to theologies of escapism. Let's look at it in context.

> Jeremiah 29:1-11
> *This is the text of the letter that the prophet Jeremiah sent from Jerusalem to the surviving elders among the exiles and to the priests, the prophets and all the other people Nebuchadnezzar had carried into exile from Jerusalem to Babylon. (This was after King Jehoiachin and the queen mother, the court officials and the leaders of Judah and Jerusalem, the skilled workers and the artisans had gone into exile from Jerusalem.) He entrusted the letter to Elasah son of Shaphan and to Gemariah son of Hilkiah, whom Zedekiah king of Judah sent to King Nebuchadnezzar in Babylon. It said: This is what the Lord Almighty, the God of Israel, says to all those I carried into exile from Jerusalem to Babylon: "Build houses and settle down; plant gardens and eat what they produce. Marry and have sons and daughters; find wives for your sons and give your daughters in marriage, so that they too may have sons and daughters. Increase in number there; do not decrease. Also, seek the peace and prosperity of the city*

> *to which I have carried you into exile. Pray to the Lord for it, because if it prospers, you too will prosper." Yes, this is what the Lord Almighty, the God of Israel, says: "Do not let the prophets and diviners among you deceive you. Do not listen to the dreams you encourage them to have. They are prophesying lies to you in my name. I have not sent them," declares the Lord. This is what the Lord says: "When seventy years are completed for Babylon, I will come to you and fulfill my good promise to bring you back to this place. For I know the plans I have for you," declares the Lord, "plans to prosper you and not to harm you, plans to give you hope and a future."*

Did you notice that the promised hope and future was in the context of being in a land that was not their own? God didn't want them to just pass through and occupy space until He would come. He commanded them to "*seek the peace and prosperity of the city to which I have carried you into.*"

He instructed them to "*build houses and settle down, plant gardens*" and produce fruit. God wanted them to redeem the city they were in.

What's remarkable about this passage is that it was written during the time of the Jewish temple. The Israelites believed that God only dwelled among them as long as they had a temple. Nebuchadnezzar had destroyed the temple, and yet here they were in a foreign land with their temple destroyed, and God was still talking to them. God's presence has never been confined to a building. His purpose has always been to be with His people wherever they are. And his intention for His people has always been to redeem cities and restore homes.

> "It is a mistake to suppose that the working classes of this country are opposed to Christianity. No one can ever be opposed to Christianity who knows what it really is…But they

> cannot follow, and must evermore live outside of, is a worship which ends with the worshiper, a religion expressed only in ceremony, and a faith unrelated to life."[17] ~Henry Drummond

I would add they also cannot follow a faith confined to a temple.

We were created to rebuild cities and restore homes. So, how do we do that? And where do we start? Drummond told us:

> You wish, you say, to be a religious man. Well, be one. There is your City; begin. But what are you to believe? Believe in your City. What else? In Jesus Christ. What about Him? That He wants to make your City better; that that is what He would be doing if He lived there. What else? Believe in yourself–that you, even you, can do some of the work which He would like done, and that unless you do it, it will remain undone. How are you to begin? As Christ did. First He looked at the City; then He wept over it; then He died for it.[18]

Henry Drummond told us to begin with our city. I could add to his thought by stating that we should each start with our own neighborhood and workplace.

As Martin Luther King told his listeners, start where you are and use what you have.

> If it is for the uplifting of humanity, it has cosmic significance, however small it is. If you are called to a little job, seek to do it in a big way. If your life's work is confined to the ordinary, seek to do it in an extraordinary way. If you discover that you are called to be a street sweeper, sweep streets like Micheal Angelo painted pictures, like Beethovan composed music, and like Shakespeare wrote poetry. Sweep streets so well that all the host of heaven and earth will have to pause and say, "here lived

a great street sweeper who swept his job well."[19]

OUR PERSONAL MISSION

Imagine if each of us, as Christians, did this. Imagine if we all started to lift humanity and sought the betterment of the places our own feet tread. If every Christian saw this as their personal mission, we would change the world. A changed world would be drawn to our King.

> "Each one of us is daily building up this City or helping to keep it back. Its walls rise slowly, but, as we believe in God, the building can never cease. For the might of those who build, be they few or many, is so surely greater than the might of those who retard, that no day's sun sets over any City in the land that does not see some stone of the invisible City laid. To believe this is faith. To live for this is Christianity."[20] ~Henry Drummond

This is a personal vision. We are all missionaries (sent ones) to our own neighborhoods, workplaces, and cities. But what about the corporate vision? What should the church of the future look like?

CHAPTER FOURTEEN

MY CITY CARE

"I saw no Temple there" —the future City will be a City without a Church. Ponder that fact, realize the temporariness of the Church, then—go and build one."
~Henry Drummond

If you don't know the purpose of something, you will abuse it. Imagine being handed a screwdriver for the first time and using it like a hammer. You would abuse both the screw and the screwdriver.

It goes without saying, but there has been a lot of abuse done by the church in the name of God. Some of that abuse is perpetrated by the *"wolves in sheeps clothing"*[1] —evil, selfish people who are intent on building their own kingdoms rather than the Kingdom of God. But I happen to believe that the majority of Christians aren't wolves. I think that most Christians today, like you and me, love Jesus and do our best to do His will.

I know I am trying my best to live for Him so that one day I will hear, *"Well done, my good and faithful servant."*[2] You too?

I believe our intentions are pure. Yet, the best intentions and 'trying hard' aren't enough. Sometimes, we abuse anyway, even when we don't mean to. Most of the time, this unintentional abuse happens because we are unclear on the purpose of things.

THE KINGDOM PURPOSE

For centuries, Christians have debated the purpose of the church. Yet, Jesus made it clear. He told His disciples, *"I have set you an example that you should do as I have done for you."*[3] And do you know what? They did.

They ministered just like Him, to the degree they were given the title Christian (Christ-like ones).

Paul, a second-generation Christian, said this, *"Follow my example, as I follow the example of Christ."*[4] He noticed that there were already abuses happening in the church in Corinth. So, he told them, "Don't do it like that. That's the wrong melody. Play it like I'm playing it." Playing the original score correctly was difficult even as early as the first century. So, let's not get too hard on ourselves when we get it wrong. Let's learn from them so we don't repeat the same mistakes. How were they getting it wrong?

He told them later on in the same chapter,

> 1 Corinthians 11:17-19
> *In the following directives I have no praise for you, for your meetings do more harm than good. In the first place, I hear that when you come together as a church, there are divisions among you, and to some extent I believe it. No doubt there have to be differences among you to show which of you have God's approval.*

Their services were doing more harm than good. There were divisions and arguments over which ones were the most right and had God's approval.

Yep, sounds like the church all right. So, how do we make sure we stay on our purpose?

We follow Jesus' example. Do as He did. Play the melody as He played it. How did He play it? *"As he approached Jerusalem and saw the city, he wept over it."*[5]

Then He died for it.

Jesus wept over the city of Jerusalem just like Nehemiah did, and just like Nehemiah, He accepted responsibility and did something about it. Yet, unlike Nehemiah, He didn't just rebuild a city. He restored an entire Kingdom by sacrificing Himself for us.

When He rose again, He instructed His disciples to focus on one city first. He didn't send them to the ends of the earth right away. He taught them to start with Jerusalem.

Yes, the same city He just wept over. Yet His solution for them wasn't to rebuild themselves. His solution was restoring a Kingdom so His ambassadors could redeem the city.

> Acts 1:8
> *"But you will receive power when the Holy Spirit comes on you; and you will be my witnesses in Jerusalem, and in all Judea and Samaria, and to the ends of the earth."*

There's a strategy here. Can you hear the original tune? Start with your city. They did.

THE KINGDOM STRATEGY

They stayed in Jerusalem, focused on one city until chapter 8 of the Book of Acts. They only left Jerusalem because of persecution. In other words, they had to be forced out.

They kept this strategy of focusing on one city at a time. In fact, we don't see denominations in the New Testament accounts. We only see city churches. The church of Corinth. The church of Ephesus. The church of Galatia. We don't see the 'First Church' of Thessalonica; we just see the church of Thessalonica.

We only know of the city churches because their objective wasn't to build temples. It was to redeem cities. Their aim was to expand the Kingdom by ministering as Jesus did, doing the work of the ministry, not just preaching it. Like Jesus, they focused on healing the sick, feeding the hungry, ministering to the poor and outcast, and loving others as Christ loved them.

Henry Drummond proclaimed a bold vision in 1893. He said:

> One Christian City, one City in any part of the earth, whose citizens from the greatest to the humblest lived in the spirit of Christ, where religion had overflowed the Churches and passed into the streets, in unandating every house and workshop, and permeating the whole social and commercial life—one such Christian City would seal the redemption of the world.[6]

Just one? I accept the challenge. Do you?

THE ORIGINAL MELODY

If you study Jesus' ministry, He spent most of His time ministering to people in the streets, not just in the Temple. Often, when Jesus entered a community, He would minister to the people's physical and emotional needs first, and then He would speak to their spiritual needs.

In my mind, no one captured Jesus' heart in this more clearly than Gregory of Nazianzus (329-390 AD). If you remember, Gregory was the friend and biographer of Bishop Basil of Caesarea, but he was also known as "the Theologian" in Eastern Orthodoxy. This is what he said of Jesus' ministry. Notice he doesn't just refer to what Jesus taught.

> He hungered—yet He fed thousands…He thirsted—yet He explained, "Whosoever thirsts, let him come to Me and drink." …He was tired—yet He is the "rest" of the weary and burdened…He prays, yet He hears prayer. He weeps, yet He puts an end to weeping…He is sold, and cheap was the price—thirty pieces of silver; yet He buys back the world at the mighty cost of His own blood. A sheep, He is led to the slaughter—yet He shepherds Israel and now the whole world as well. A lamb, He is dumb—yet He is the "Word" …He is weakened, wounded—yet He cures every disease and every weakness. He is brought up to the tree and nailed to it—yet by the tree of life He restores us…He is given vinegar to drink, gall to eat—and who is He? Why, one who turned water into wine, who took away the taste of bitterness, who is all sweetness and desire. He surrenders His life, yet He has power to take it again. He dies, but He vivifies and by death destroys death. He is buried, yet rises again.[7]

That's our King! In this, you can hear the original melody, and it is beautiful!

The disciples and the early church leadership seemed as inspired by Jesus' actions as they were by His words. In particular, they were inspired by His ministry to the *"least of these."*[8]

Gregory was so inspired by how Jesus ministered that he wrote the most precise purpose statement I have ever read for the church. But first, he acknowledged how difficult it is to discover the original purpose as designed by Jesus:

> It is not at all an easy task to discover the one virtue that surpasses all others and to give it the scepter and palm, just as it is not easy in a meadow fragrant with many blossoms to find the most fragrant and beautiful.[9]

He was digging for the original score written by Jesus. He was looking for the one thing to anchor the purpose of the church on. After considering many of the Christian virtues, he concluded that:

> following Paul and Christ himself, we must regard charity as the first and greatest of the commandments since it is the very sum of the Law and the Prophets, [and] its most vital part I find is the love of the poor...[10]

There we have it. A clear purpose. When we make other things more important than charity, particularly our ministry to the poor, we play a different tune than Jesus wrote.

Robin Lane Fox, an English historian, wrote of this focus in the early church. He said in his book, *Pagans and Christians*, "To the poor, the widows and orphans, Christians gave alms and support, like the synagogue communities, their forerunners. This 'brotherly' love has been minimized as a reason for turning to the Church, as if only those who were members could know of it. In fact, it is widely recognized...Christian 'love' was public knowledge and must have played its part in drawing outsiders to the faith."[11]

The result of playing the tune right is that it draws 'outsiders to the faith.' When the tune is played right, it is beautiful.

We can no longer make excuses for lack of clarity about our purpose. It is clear. Love as Jesus loved. Minister to the "least of these," starting in our own city.

THE BIG 6

Jesus said we will give an account on the Day of Judgment, not just for what we believe, but for what we do. He told His disciple this clearly, and they believed Him. So should we.

Matthew 25:34-40

"Then the King will say to those on his right, 'Come, you who are blessed by my Father; take your inheritance, the kingdom prepared for you since the creation of the world. For I was hungry and you gave me something to eat, I was thirsty and you gave me something to drink, I was a stranger and you invited me in, I needed clothes and you clothed me, I was sick and you looked after me, I was in prison and you came to visit me.' "Then the righteous will answer him, 'Lord, when did we see you hungry and feed you, or thirsty and give you something to drink? When did we see you a stranger and invite you in, or needing clothes and clothe you? When did we see you sick or in prison and go to visit you?' "The King will reply, 'Truly I tell you, whatever you did for one of the least of these brothers and sisters of mine, you did for me.'

If we have any questions about where we should start ministering charity in our cities, Jesus listed six primary needs for us to focus on:

1. Food
2. Water
3. Housing
4. Clothing
5. Health
6. Justice

Two thousand years later, these six are still the most significant needs on the planet today. I would venture to guess that these six still categorize the greatest needs in your local community as well.

What if the church of the city decided to take care of these needs instead of expecting the governments or agencies to take care of them?

Jesus didn't delegate these needs to the government, the Red Cross, or any other agency. He was talking to His followers. He expects us, as His representatives on earth, to meet these needs. To abdicate these needs to someone else is to risk being cast away by Him for eternity.

> Matthew 25:41-46
> *"Then he will say to those on his left, 'Depart from me, you who are cursed, into the eternal fire prepared for the devil and his angels. For I was hungry and you gave me nothing to eat, I was thirsty and you gave me nothing to drink, I was a stranger and you did not invite me in, I needed clothes and you did not clothe me, I was sick and in prison and you did not look after me.' "They also will answer, 'Lord, when did we see you hungry or thirsty or a stranger or needing clothes or sick or in prison, and did not help you?' "He will reply, 'Truly I tell you, whatever you did not do for one of the least of these, you did not do for me.' "Then they will go away to eternal punishment, but the righteous to eternal life."*

The disciples and the early church leaders took this warning seriously, and I believe you and I should also. This is not a "good idea" and a gentle suggestion. This is a command from our King.

WHY AREN'T WE DOING OUR JOB?

We, as Christians, haven't acted on this expectation for only a few reasons. Number one, we were naive. We didn't know this was expected of us, just like the ones Jesus discussed in verse 44. This expectation came as a surprise. No one told us this was such a big deal.

Being naive was not a valid excuse for those Jesus talked about in Matthew 25. They were still cast out. It's not an acceptable excuse for us, either. We have read these scriptures, and now we know. In addition, the fact that you have gotten this far in the book means you can no longer claim naivety.

The second reason we have not acted on this expectation is that we are playing the fool. A fool knows better yet chooses to ignore the truth anyway. Jesus said there would be those like this. Don't be a fool.

Thirdly, and this is the one I struggle with the most. We have succumbed to our excuses.

Some of the more common excuses as to why we aren't helping the "least of these" are:

1. **"I don't see any needs around me."**
   It is easy for us to look at the surface of our affluent communities and imagine there is no one struggling to put food on the table, homeless, unable to access healthcare or clothe themselves or their kids. Well, I urge you to look more closely at your community. There are enormous needs around you.
   Did you know that 37.2 million people are living in poverty in the United States right now?[12] There are 4.9 million, or one individual for every seven, living in poverty in Canada.[13] Did you know that there are currently an estimated 552,830 homeless people in the US,[14] and 235,000 homeless in Canada?[15]
   We can't be blind to that.

2. **"Others are doing a better job of meeting their needs."**
   If you see someone meeting a need with excellence, great! Join them. I have yet to meet a social agency anywhere that doesn't need more volunteers and couldn't use more money. I think all the social services in the world should be largely staffed with Christian volunteers. We don't have to run every agency, but we can't afford to sit on the sidelines either. Pick one of the above six needs, and find out if someone is

meeting that need in your community. If you find one that is, join them. If you don't, start a ministry to meet the need.

3. **"It's too expensive."**
We can make this excuse as individuals thinking that we don't have any extra money to help, or we can make this excuse as churches thinking that we have so many other ministries we need to support that we couldn't possibly do anymore. I get it. I do.
However, if you are making more than $30,000 per year, you are among the top 93% of the wealthiest people in the world. It's not a matter of not having enough. It's the lifestyle we choose to live. We could all cut a few things out in our spending to free up some margin to help those less fortunate than ourselves.
Did you know that Christians make up 33% of the world's population but receive 53% of the world's annual income and spend 98% of it on themselves?[16] Christian's annual income is $12.3 trillion. $213 billion is given to Christian causes. $11.4 billion is given to foreign missions, 87% of which goes to work being done among the already Christian, 12% goes to work among the evangelized non-Christians, and 1% among the unevangelized.[17]
One percent. I think we can do better, don't you?

4. **"If I help, it'll just enable them."**
This quick, dismissive thought allows us to leave guilt-free. But hold on, Jesus didn't leave room for excuses in Matthew 25. He just expected us to help.
We often make this excuse when someone on the street asks us for money, as they might use that money and spend it on alcohol or drugs, but they might not. Also, if you feel

uncomfortable giving cash, why don't you buy them a meal or offer them a grocery card or some other tangible gift?

5. **"I don't have time."**
   You'll have lots of time in "eternal punishment" to think about how you were too busy to help.
   Sorry, too far?
   We don't have time; we make it. How we spend time is always a choice.

6. **"It's not my gift or calling."**
   I'll let William Booth, the founder of the Salvation Army, answer this one. He said, "'Not called!' did you say? 'Not heard the call,' I think you should say. Put your ear down to the Bible, and hear Him bid you go and pull sinners out of the fire of sin. Put your ear down to the burdened, agonized heart of humanity and listen to its pitiful wail for help. Go stand by the gates of hell, and hear the damned entreat you to go to their father's house and bid their brothers and sisters and servants and masters not to come there. Then, look Christ in the face—whose mercy you have professed to obey—and tell Him whether you will join heart and soul and body and circumstances in the march to publish His mercy to the world."[18]

7. **"But I'm praying for them."**
   Prayer is great. Don't stop praying, but it is not enough. When we say we are praying, it is often used as an excuse to not have to roll up our sleeves to help. Plus, when we only pray, we are actually casting all of the responsibility on God to solve the problem.
   Nehemiah didn't just pray and ask God to solve his problems.

He prayed and asked God for the opportunity to solve the problem himself. We are to be the hands and feet of Jesus. This is our territory. We can't use prayer as an excuse. The persecuted church didn't only pray. They had every excuse to hide away and not help those in need, but they chose to act.

1 Peter 4:7-10 (NLT)
The end of the world is coming soon. Therefore, be earnest and disciplined in your prayers. Most important of all, continue to show deep love for each other, for love covers a multitude of sins. Cheerfully share your home with those who need a meal or a place to stay.

Did you see that? Peter said, most important of all. That sounds like a big deal to me. He said that there was something else more important than their earnest and disciplined prayer life, it was showing deep love for each other and showing hospitality and feeding the hungry.

These seven are just some of the more common excuses we can make to justify why we are abdicating our duties as ambassadors of the King in our communities. I am sure there are more.

What are some of your most common excuses for not activating your faith in this way? Call them out. If you're like me, the moment you speak them out loud, you realize how lame and weak they are. There is no excuse for us not obeying our King's command.

HOW TO DISCOVER YOUR PURPOSE

Let's go back to the "calling" one. What is your purpose in life? Why are you here? What is your specific calling? Have you found it difficult to answer those questions confidently? Well, I have good news for you! Your purpose and calling are hidden within a problem to solve. Instead of escaping from problems with excuses, pray for ways you can become the solution.

Nehemiah discovered his purpose when he heard the report of the state of his city. He didn't ask God if he should. He didn't even ask God to fix it or send someone else. It was a problem to solve. Nehemiah, not taking into account his own abilities or lack of experience, rose to the occasion. All he did was see a problem and move toward solving it. God did the rest.

Hey Christians! Stop waiting for God to bring revival. Find a problem in your city and ask God for the opportunity to become the solution. Then, go to work solving it. Don't wait. Go.

The only time Jesus instructed the church to wait was when he asked the disciples to wait in Jerusalem until they received the Holy Spirit. Once they received Him, they immediately left the upper room and went to work redeeming Jerusalem. We have access to the same Holy Spirit right now. If you have already received Him, you have all you need to bring revival to your city, too. You don't need to wait for God to move. God has given us the authority here. He's waiting for us to move.

Hey, Christian businessman or woman! You know this already. Find a problem in your city and solve it with the utmost excellence. Build the best business you can build. But remember, you're not building a personal castle. You're called to build the Kingdom. How can your business solve problems in your city that will clarify which King you serve?

Hey, employees! Your calling is hidden within a problem to solve. So, what problem do you see at work that you could solve with excellence? You will have no issue with being promoted and paid well if you become an invaluable problem solver in your company.

Hey, students! You're not too young to find problems and solve them. What problem do you see at school that you could solve?

Christians don't run from problems. We run to them. We were made on purpose, for a purpose, for such a time as this. Jesus didn't put an age limit on who should minister to the "least of these." That is something we all can do regardless of age or experience.

Hey, pastor! You're not called to grow a church. That's not your problem to solve. You won't give God an account for your church attendance on the day of Judgment. I'll repeat it: you're not called to grow a church. You're called to equip the saints for the work of their ministry. Equip means 'to skill develop.' So, you are called to develop the skills of those in your congregation to solve problems in your city. You are also called to lead your church to become the beacon of hope for the "least of these" in your city.

This is why we started a ministry in our church called MyCityCare. It's a ministry designed to bring care to the "least of these" in our city. We currently have churches in 5 communities. Each congregation operates a MyCityCare because we want each church to be the "city on a hill, " a beacon of hope to the community. You guessed it, MyCityCare is based on Matthew 25 and seeks to meet the six specific needs Jesus listed.

The cities we are in that already have food banks; we partner with those food banks to feed the hungry. In the communities that don't have a food bank, we have become the food bank.

We have active members of our church working for ministries that drill wells and provide fresh water to those who do not have access to such amenities. This is happening overseas, but we are actively working on providing water ministries locally as well. We have recently become aware of a major problem in Canada in this area. While there has been progress in the past seven years, there are still 36 long-term drinking water advisories on First Nation reserves. Some of these advisories have been in place for over 25 years. There is also a deficit in funding for the maintenance and operation of drinking water systems on reserves, which the Parliamentary Budget

Officer identified as being $138 million annually.[19] There are many legalities to jump through before we can meet this need, but we have identified a problem and are seeking a solution.

That's all it takes, pastor: find a problem and look for opportunities to solve it. Be careful not to allow excuses to steal your opportunity.

Our MyCityCare ministries hand out clothing daily through Street Stores and projects like our Cinderella Project, which provides gowns and tuxedos for graduating high school seniors who wouldn't necessarily be able to afford one. We set up miniature clothing stores and provide personal shopping experiences so that each student is treated with the utmost dignity.

We are currently building affordable housing in our city. We are active in rescuing underaged girls and boys from sex trafficking as our justice arm. I am watching and praying for an opportunity to become a solution in healthcare.

I say all of this not to brag but instead to say that I have been highly convicted that I have pastored for over 20 years and did not make these things my main focus. I have sought to build a large church and saw that as my calling. I was good at it, but the COVID-19 pandemic caused me to question everything and study the church's history deeper. I am now convinced to the core of my being that as an ambassador of the King, I'm not called to build castles. I'm called to expand the Kingdom of God by ministering to the "least of these."

And you are, too. I hope you see that now.

SEE A NEED MEET A NEED

I am inspired by pastors like Tim Lucas and his church Liquid Church in New Jersey, who saw a massive need and sought to meet it. Pastor Tim said, "Medical debt is tied to two-thirds of bankruptcies in America, and it ruins credit for families, impacting their ability to secure housing, car loans, job opportunities, and more. Our church had a heart to give some fresh hope to our neighbors in need. We want them to have a clean slate to start 2021, and to remind them that they're loved and God has not forgotten them."

How did they help? They gave over $13.7 million and eliminated 3800 families' medical debt.[20]

In the same year, Liquid Church heard of another major need. The church responded to a report sent out by the U.S. State Department regarding an emergency in Haiti. Seeing the need, the church rallied over 3000 volunteers and packed 1.1 million meals that were sent to Haiti.[21]

Come on! Isn't that amazing?

You might think there is no way that you or your church could respond to that degree, but you don't need to do things that significant to make a difference. The point I want to make here is simply this: See a need—meet a need.

Henry Drummond said:

> To move among the people on the common street; to meet them in the market-place on equal terms; to live among them not as saint or monk, but as brother-man with brother man; to serve God not with form or ritual, but in the free impulse of a soul; to bear the burdens of society and relieve its needs; to carry on the multitudinous activities of the city—social, commercial, political, philanthropic—in Christ's spirit and for His ends; this is the religion of the Son of Man, and the only meetness for Heaven which has much reality in it.[22]

When Christians fail to engage the world and change it for the better, they fail to be the church. Let's take our job back.

CONCLUSION

I hope you now recognize the difference between the beautiful score Jesus wrote for the church and the one currently being played. If you haven't, the world has.

Missiologist Ralph D. Winter noted the difference. He claimed, "In AD 100, there were 12 unreached people groups for every congregation of believers. Now there is one unreached people group for every 1000 congregations."[1]

In many ways, the global church is doing well. I don't mean to dismiss what is working. However, we are a long way from where we could be, especially when I see the state of the world and the general response of Christians. Most of the church seems to be looking up, waiting for Jesus to return, instead of looking around and bringing Jesus to the world. I am excited for Jesus to return, too, but before the King returns, we should make the colony much more presentable for Him.

We have work to do!

Nehemiah received a bad report of the state of his city. He

responded to that report by accepting personal and corporate responsibility. He didn't cast the blame on God. He didn't expect the king to repair it himself. He didn't make excuses as to why he couldn't respond. He accepted responsibility, which gave him the ability to respond.

We need to look at the church's report and respond in the same way. We can't blame God or wait idly for Him to move. We can't cast blame on all of the other denominations, pastors, leaders, and Christians for giving us a bad name. We can't make excuses as to why we aren't the ones to respond. We need to accept personal and corporate responsibility.

I AND MY FATHERS HAVE SINNED.

We have made Christianity a personal faith, not a social one. We have hidden our light under a basket called the church and reduced our worship to a temple. We have created a faith without works, and it is dead. It's dead to the world and has become resistible and, in some cases, repulsive.

We have abdicated our responsibilities and allowed governments and agencies to minister to the "least of these" more effectively than us. We have shifted our attention from the needs of our communities to our personal preferences. We have focused more on being right than doing right. This shift in focus has led to divisions among us and the creation of strange theologies.

We have made excuses as to why the problems we see in the world are not within our capability or responsibility to solve. We have focused on escaping this cruel world to such a degree that we have missed our purpose and calling to be the light in the darkness.

Sin means to miss the bullseye. We have failed to balance grace and truth, faith and wisdom, love and impact, authority and power. We have not perfectly balanced our personal ambition, care for others, and relationship with God. We have allowed command, control, and coin to entice us to compromise and corruption.

We take responsibility for our jobs to give ourselves the ability to take our job back.

WE ARE KINGDOM PEOPLE

Nehemiah didn't just take responsibility. He also knew his identity. He gave himself the courage to respond by anchoring himself in his identity. We do the same.

We were created on purpose, for a purpose, for such a time as this. We are sons and daughters of God. We are ambassadors on earth representing the King and His Kingdom. We have been given the authority and the power to rule this domain. This colony is our responsibility. If it is dark, it's because we aren't being the light. If it is broken, it's because we haven't provided solutions. If it is hurting, it is because we haven't provided care. As Augustine said, "Without God, we cannot. Without us, God will not."

We are the rebuilder of cities and the restorer of homes. As Henry Drummond said, "To make good Cities—that is for the present hour the main work of Christianity."[2]

We know who we are and the authority and power we have.

WE ARE THE SOLUTION

Nehemiah didn't pray and ask God for a solution; he prayed and asked God for the opportunity to be the solution.

We see the state of our world. We are not seeking to escape. We will not abdicate our responsibilities. We will be the light, keeping our lampstand in its proper position. We will minister to the "least of these." We will love each other as Christ has loved us. We will out-love, out-serve, and out-give everyone, everywhere, every time.

Just imagine with me. What if denominations chose to accept personal and corporate responsibility, choosing to love and serve? Imagine if they decided to serve their local churches instead of asking their churches to serve them. Imagine if they raised the banner of the Kingdom higher than the banner of their own castles. Imagine if they equipped their churches to reach their cities.

What if churches chose to accept personal and corporate responsibility? Imagine if they decided to serve their people instead of asking their people to serve them. Imagine if they cared for their people so much that there was no need among them. Imagine if they equipped their people and released them as missionaries to reach their city. Imagine if they raised the Kingdom's banner higher than their castle's banner. Imagine if, instead of building their own ministry, they chose to build their city.

What if Christians chose to accept personal and corporate responsibility? What if they loved each other like Jesus loved them? What if they decided to out-love, out-serve, and out-give everyone they met? Imagine if they valued being one over being right. Imagine if they chose to fight for the "least of these" instead of fighting each other and took the stance of William Booth.

> While women weep, as they do now, I'll fight; while children go hungry, as they do now, I'll fight; while men go to prison, in and out, in and out, as they do now, I'll fight; while there is a drunkard left, while there is a poor lost girl upon the streets, while there remains one dark soul without the light of God, I'll fight—I'll fight to the very end![3]

What would be the result if most of us chose to accept responsibility, got anchored in our Kingdom identity, and decided to be the solution, focusing on rebuilding cities and restoring homes?

Revival.

Society would find the church irresistible once again. As Henry Drummond said, "The masses will never return to the Church till its true relation to the City is more defined."[4]

Well, we're defining it. We are taking responsibility for our city. We know our identity. We are the solution.

Let's take our job back.

ENDNOTES

THE STATE OF THE UNION

1. https://www.cnn.com/2020/03/11/health/coronavirus-pandemic-world-health-organization/index.html
2. Henry Drummond, *The City Without a Church*,
3. https://en.wikipedia.org/wiki/Murder_of_George_Floyd#cite_note-auto-184
4. https://www.christianitytoday.com/news/2020/june/pastors-george-floyd-racism-church-barna-research.html
5. https://www.nytimes.com/2022/04/25/us/politics/evangelical-churches-trump-election.html
6. https://globalnews.ca/news/7607091/us-capitol-riot-christianity-questions
7. https://globalnews.ca/news/7607091/us-capitol-riot-christianity-questions/
8. https://www.christianitytoday.com/ct/2022/january-web-only/january-6-attack-russell-moore-post-christian-church.html

9. Gerald Sittser, *Resilient Faith*, 7
10. Gerald Sittser, *Resilient Faith*, 178
11. https://apnews.com/article/canada-982aae1a74c8ca266abe0f737e4afa4c
12. https://www.facinghistory.org/stolen-lives-indigenous-peoples-canada-and-indian-residential-schools/chapter-3/role-churches
13. Luke 18:14
14. Gerald Sittser, *Resilient Faith*, 13
15. https://www.covenantchristian.net/blog/inscribing-scripture-on-your-childs-heart#:~:text=In%20traditional%20Jewish%20education%2C%20students,an%20assortment%20of%20memorization%20methods.

WHO IS TO BLAME?

1. https://www.crosswalk.com/faith/bible-study/what-is-sin-5-things-that-may-surprise-you.html
2. Isaiah 58:13
3. James 2:19-20
4. https://en.wikipedia.org/wiki/Ninety-five_Theses#cite_note-FOOTNOTEBrecht1985178-11
5. https://en.wikipedia.org/wiki/Indulgence#cite_note-Modern_Guide-1
6. https://en.wikipedia.org/wiki/Indulgence#cite_note-vatican.va-2
7. https://en.wikipedia.org/wiki/Ninety-five_Theses#cite_note-FOOTNOTEBrecht1985180-12
8. https://en.wikipedia.org/wiki/Ninety-five_Theses#cite_note-FOOTNOTEBrecht1985183-13
9. https://en.wikipedia.org/wiki/Ninety-five_Theses#cite_note-FOOTNOTEBrecht1985184-17
10. https://en.wikipedia.org/wiki/Theology_of_Martin_Luther#cite_note-1
11. https://en.wikipedia.org/wiki/Sola_gratia#cite_note-Rublack2017-3
12. https://en.wikipedia.org/wiki/Ninety-five_Theses#cite_note-

FOOTNOTEBrecht1985195-26

13. https://www.registerguard.com/story/lifestyle/faith/2020/03/13/looper-column-curious-origin-word/984185007/
14. Ed Silvoso, *Ekklesia*, 25
15. https://en.wikipedia.org/wiki/William_Tyndale#cite_note-FOOTNOTEMoynahan200372-59
16. https://en.wikipedia.org/wiki/William_Tyndale#cite_note-FOOTNOTEHarding201228-58
17. https://en.wikipedia.org/wiki/William_Tyndale#cite_note-FOOTNOTEFoxe1570[httpwwwhrionlineacukjohnfoxemain8_1570_1228jsp_VIII.1228]-38
18. https://en.wikipedia.org/wiki/William_Tyndale#cite_note-FOOTNOTEDaniell2001383-41
19. https://en.wikipedia.org/wiki/William_Tyndale#cite_note-FOOTNOTEMoynahan20031%E2%80%932-61
20. Ed Silvoso, *Ekklesia*, 43
21. Martin Luther King, *"The Three Dimensions of a Complete Life,"* 24 January 1954.

WHAT DID THE EARLY CHURCH DO?

1. Pliny, Letters 10.96 (Radice, Loeb Classical Library 59), 285-291.
2. Tertullian, *Apology*, 42.
3. Pliny, Letters 10.96 (Radice, Loeb Classical Library 59), 285-291.
4. Pliny, Letters 10.96 (Radice, Loeb Classical Library 59), 285-291.
5. Pliny, Letters 10.96 (Radice, Loeb Classical Library 59), 285-291.
6. Pliny, Letters 10.96 (Radice, Loeb Classical Library 59), 285-291.
7. Pliny, Letters 10.96 (Radice, Loeb Classical Library 59), 291-293.
8. Ignatius, Ephesians, 10.1-3 (Holmes, Apostolic Fathers), 191-192.
9. Michael Holmes, *The Apostolic Fathers: Greek Texts and English Translations* (Grand Rapids: Baker Academic, 2007), 166-271
10. Justin Martyr, *First Apology 67*, in ANF 1:186
11. Tertullian, *To Scapula*, 1-2 (Thewall, The Ante-Nicene Fathers.)

12. Tertullian, *Apology* 39, in ANF 3:46
13. The So-Called Letter to Diognetus 10.6, in Richardson, ECF, 221
14. The So-Called Letter to Diognetus 10.6, in Richardson, ECF, 221
15. https://www.worldhistory.org/article/992/plague-of-cyprian-250-270-ce/
16. Eusebius, Hist.,237.
17. Pontius, *Life of St. Cyprian*, 9-10.
18. Pontius, *Life of St. Cyprian,* 10.
19. Epistle of Dionysius, in *Eusebius, Ecclesiastical History* 7.22.7-9 (Oulton, Loeb Classical Library 265). Archaic English adjusted in consultation with the Greek text.
20. Eusebius, Hist. 7.22, 237.
21. Quoted in Rodney Stark, *the Rise of Christianity* (Princeton: Princeton University Press, 1996), 104.
22. Letter to Arsacius, High-priest of Galatia, in *The Works of the Emperor Julian*, vol. 3, ed. Wilmer Cave Wright (New York: Putnam's Sons, 1923), 67.
23. Julian, *Fragment of a Letter to a Priest* 305b–d (Wright, Loeb Classical Library 29), 337-339.
24. Julian, *Misopogon ("Beard-hater")* 363a (Wright, Loeb Classical Library 29), 491.

CONSTANTINE CHANGED EVERYTHING

1. The Edict of Milan is preserved in *Lactantius, The Death of the Persecutors* 48 (McDonald, Lactantius, The Minor Works). Another version of the edict is found in Eusebius, Ecclesiastical History 10.5. On the details of the edict, its sources, meaning, and significance, see Milton Anastos, "*The Edict of Milan (313): A Defence of its Traditional Authorship and Designation,*" Revue des etudes byzantines 25 (1967):13-41
2. https://earlychurchhistory.org/medicine/infanticide-in-the-ancient-world/

3. Seneca, De ira, *The Third Book of the Dialogues of L/ Annaesus Seneca,* book 1, section 15, trans. Aubrey Stewart, http://en.wikisource.org/wiki/Of_Anger/Book_1#1.
4. Aristotle, Politics 7.14.10 (Rackham, Loeb Classical Library 264), 623.
5. https://earlychurchhistory.org/medicine/infanticide-in-the-ancient-world/
6. Theodosian Code 11.27.1-2 (Phar, The Theodosian Code).
7. See Nathan, *The Family in Late Antiquity*, 66. Eusebius, *Life of Constantine* 4.28.
8. Theodosian Code 16.2.4 (Phar, The Theodosian Code).
9. Theodosian Code 16.2.6 (Phar, The Theodosian Code).
10. John Dickson, *Bullies and Saints*, 84.
11. https://en.wikipedia.org/wiki/Basil_of_Caesarea#cite_note-McSorley-27
12. https://www.newadvent.org/fathers/310243.htm
13. Gregory of Nazianzus, *The Panegyric of Saint Basil*, in NPNYF27: 416-417.
14. https://aggos.com/news/82439
15. Gregory of Nazianzus, T*he Panegyric of Saint Basil*, in NPNYF27: 416-417.
16. Ferngren, *Medicine and Health Care in Early Christianity*, 129.
17. https://en.wikipedia.org/wiki/Basil_of_Caesarea#cite_note-38
18. Jerome, *"On the Death of Fabiola,"* Letter 77.6 (Wright, Loeb Classical Library 262), 323. Jerome's two letters to Fabiola are no. 64 and no. 78.
19. Gregory of Nyssa, *Life of Macrina*, 26.30. See Judith Evans Grubbs, *"Church, State, and Children: Christian and Imperial Attitudes Toward Infant Exposure in Late Antiquity,"* in *The Power of Religion in Late Antiquity,* ed. Andrew Cain and Noel Lenski (New York: Routledge, 2009), 128-29.
20. https://en.wikipedia.org/wiki/Apostolic_Constitutions
21. Constitutions of Holy Apostles 4.1.2. In ANF 7: 433.
22. https://www.newadvent.org/fathers/3815.htm

23. https://en.wikipedia.org/wiki/Ambrose#cite_note-FOOTNOTEButler1991407-31
24. https://en.wikipedia.org/wiki/Ambrose
25. Brown, *Eye of a Needle,* 527-528.
26. Brown, *Eye of a Needle*, 122.
27. John Dickson, *Bullies and Saints*, 105.

MOVEMENTS VS. ORGANIZATIONS

1. https://ssir.org/articles/entry/building_movements_not_organizations
2. https://www.newadvent.org/cathen/08558b.htm
3. Translation from the site earlychurchtexts.com
4. Theodosian Code, 16.10.11 (Phar, The Theodosian Code).
5. https://en.wikipedia.org/wiki/Library_of_Alexandria#cite_note-FOOTNOTEWatts2008191-111
6. https://en.wikipedia.org/wiki/Sack_of_Rome_(410)#cite_note-Jerome127-2
7. https://en.wikipedia.org/wiki/Sack_of_Rome_(410)#cite_note-85
8. https://en.wikipedia.org/wiki/Sack_of_Rome_(410)#cite_note-102
9. https://en.wikipedia.org/wiki/The_City_of_God
10. https://web.archive.org/web/20130725190746/http://etext.lib.virginia.edu/etcbin/toccer-new2id=AugCity.xml&images=images%2Fmodeng&data= %2Ftexts%2Fenglish%2Fmodeng%2Fparsed&tag=public&part=all Augustine, *The City of God,* Book XIX Chapter 7
11. https://ssir.org/articles/entry/building_movements_not_organizations
12. Henry Chadwick, *Augustine: A Very Short Introduction* (Oxford: Oxford University Press, 1986), 112-13.
13. https://ssir.org/articles/entry/building_movements_not_organizations
14. https://stmichaelsgeneva.org/timelineofchurchhistory
15. Peter J. Heather, "*Theoderic,*" Oxford Classical Dictionary, 1499.
16. https://en.wikipedia.org/wiki/Code_of_Justinian#cite_note-5
17. https://en.wikipedia.org/wiki/Code_of_Justinian#cite_note-10

18. https://www.ijhssnet.com/journals/Vol_7_No_1_January_2017/7.pdf
19. https://www.ijhssnet.com/journals/Vol_7_No_1_January_2017/7.pdf
20. https://en.wikipedia.org/wiki/Holy_Roman_Empire#:~:text=On%2025%20December%20800%2C%20Pope,Western%20Roman%20Empire%20in%20476
21. https://en.wikipedia.org/wiki/Holy_Roman_Empire#:~:text=On%2025%20December%20800%2C%20Pope,Western%20Roman%20Empire%20in%20476
22. https://en.wikipedia.org/wiki/Holy_Roman_Empire#:~:text=On%2025%20December%20800%2C%20Pope,Western%20Roman%20Empire%20in%20476E
23. https://en.wikipedia.org/wiki/Imperial_church_system#cite_note-Bejcz%C3%BD-1
24. https://en.wikipedia.org/wiki/Imperial_church_system#cite_note-pavlott-3
25. https://en.wikipedia.org/wiki/Papal_primacy#cite_note-FOOTNOTEPhan2000486%E2%80%93488-7
26. https://en.wikipedia.org/wiki/Holy_Roman_Empire#cite_note-FOOTNOTEBarraclough1984122%E2%80%93124-97
27. https://en.wikipedia.org/wiki/Holy_Roman_Empire#:~:text=On%2025%20December%20800%2C%20Pope,Western%20Roman%20Empire%20in%20476
28. https://en.wikipedia.org/wiki/Holy_Roman_Empire#:~:text=On%2025%20December%20800%2C%20Pope,Western%20Roman%20Empire%20in%20476
29. John 18:36
30. Dr. Stuart Murray, *Post-Christendom*, 76-78

JESUS IS KING

1. Nehemiah 1:10

2. Matthew 6:33
3. Matthew 4:23
4. Matthew 24:3
5. John 16:14-15

ON EARTH AS IT IS IN HEAVEN

1. Genesis 1:1
2. https://www.worldatlas.com/articles/who-owns-all-the-land-in-canada.html#:~:text=The%20land%20of%20Canada%20is,of%20the%20government%20of%20Canada.
3. Myles Monroe; *Kingdom Principles*, 62.
4. https://www.worldatlas.com/articles/who-owns-all-the-land-in-canada.html#:~:text=The%20land%20of%20Canada%20is,of%20the%20government%20of%20Canada.
5. https://www.merriam-webster.com/dictionary/colony
6. Philippians 3:20
7. Myles Monroe, *Kingdom Principles*, 65-66.
8. Matthew 4:17 (Msg)
9. https://en.wikipedia.org/wiki/Transfer_of_the_Portuguese_court_to_Brazil#cite_note-dean-3
10. https://en.wikipedia.org/wiki/Transfer_of_the_Portuguese_court_to_Brazil#cite_note-dean-3
11. https://work.chron.com/general-duties-ambassador-17594.html
12. Joshua 5:13-14 (Msg)
13. John 13:34
14. Matthew 25:40
15. Nehemiah 1:6
16. Nehemiah 2:8

BIG GOVERNMENT

1. Myles Monroe, *Kingdom Principles*, 43.
2. https://en.wikipedia.org/wiki/Feudalism#cite_note-39

3. https://en.wikipedia.org/wiki/Dictatorship
4. https://en.wikipedia.org/wiki/Plato%27s_five_regimes#cite_note-2
5. Luke 9:23

DON'T MOVE THE LAMPSTAND

1. N.T. Wright, *Revelation for Everyone*, 13
2. John Stott, *What Christ Thinks of the Church*, 87

IDENTITY CRISIS

1. https://cae.appstate.edu/sites/cae.appstate.edu/files/big-8-identities.pdf
2. https://www.healthline.com/health/different-genders
3. https://relevantmagazine.com/faith/where-christian-name-really-came/
4. https://www.vvdailypress.com/story/lifestyle/faith/2016/08/26/why-did-gandhi-say-x2018/985856007/
5. https://www.mkgandhi.org/articles/christ&g.htm
6. https://en.wikipedia.org/wiki/Arianism#cite_note-FOOTNOTECarroll198712-18
7. https://en.wikipedia.org/wiki/East%E2%80%93West_Schism#cite_note-FOOTNOTELembke2010-9
8. https://en.wikipedia.org/wiki/Western_Schism#cite_note-2
9. https://www.livescience.com/christianity-denominations.html
10. https://www.livescience.com/christianity-denominations.html
11. https://www.livescience.com/christianity-denominations.html
12. https://www.livescience.com/christianity-denominations.html

ABDICATED RESPONSIBILITIES

1. https://bibleapps.com/greek/3404.htm
2. Stark, *The Rise of Christianity*, 5-7. This calculation seems to be made using various accepted sources. These sources include the widely accepted figures for the year 200 and year 300. With this information Stark estimated an 43% growth rate per decade.)
3. https://en.wikipedia.org/wiki/Plague_of_Cyprian#cite_note-7

4. Epistle of Dionysius, in Eusebius, Ecclesiastical History 7.22.7-9 (Oulton, Loeb Classical Library 265). Archaic English adjusted in consultation with the Greek text.
5. Dr. Myles Monroe, *Rediscovering the Kingdom*, 146
6. https://en.wikipedia.org/wiki/Plague_of_Cyprian#cite_note-harperCh4-2
7. https://en.wikipedia.org/wiki/Basil_of_Caesarea
8. Geunter B. Risse, *Mending Bodies, Saving Souls: A History of Hospitals* (Oxford: Oxford University Press, 1999), 73
9. https://en.wikipedia.org/wiki/History_of_hospitals#cite_note-Catholic-13
10. John S. Dickerson, *Jesus Skeptic*, 112.
11. https://en.wikipedia.org/wiki/Edward_Jenner#cite_note-JennerBBC-7
12. https://en.wikipedia.org/wiki/Smallpox#cite_note-99
13. John Baron, *The Life of Edward Jenner: With Illustrations of His Doctrines, and Selections from His Correspondence* (London: Henry Colburn, 1838), 2:295.
14. https://en.wikipedia.org/wiki/Florence_Nightingale#cite_note-26
15. https://en.wikipedia.org/wiki/Florence_Nightingale#cite_note-26
16. Lynn McDonald, ed., *Florence Nightingale's Suggestions for Thought* (Waterloo, ON: Wilfrid Laurier University Press, 2008), 11:96.
17. John S. Dickerson, *Jesus Skeptic*, 122-123.
18. https://en.wikipedia.org/wiki/Mayo_Clinic#cite_note-45
19. https://en.wikipedia.org/wiki/Mary_Alfred_Moes#cite_note-5
20. John S. Dickerson, *Jesus Skeptic*, pg 120.
21. https://en.wikipedia.org/wiki/Catechetical_School_of_Alexandria
22. https://en.wikipedia.org/wiki/Monastic_school#cite_note-Kottje_1999-1
23. https://en.wikipedia.org/wiki/University_of_Oxford
24. Rodney Stark, *For the Glory of God*, 121-201.
25. John S. Dickerson, *Jesus Skeptic*, 54-56.
26. Isaac Newton, *Philosophiae Naturalis Principia Mathematica*

(Mathematical Principles of Natural Philosophy) (1687).
27. https://www.spindleworks.com/library/rfaber/luther_edu.htm
28. https://en.wikipedia.org/wiki/Johannes_Sturm
29. Michael D. Waggoner and Nathan C. Walker, eds., *The Oxford Handbook of Religion and American Education* (Oxford: Oxford University Press, 2018), 170.
30. https://en.wikipedia.org/wiki/Massachusetts_School_Laws#cite_note-3
31. Donald Tewksbury, The Founding of American Colleges and Universities before the Civil War (1932), citied in Alvin J. Schmidt, *How Christianity Changed the World* (Grand Rapids: Zondervan, 2001), 190.
32. https://www.ajc.com/blog/get-schooled/higher-education-biased-against-traditional-christians/OvUZDRhTjVTpPIb3oa9ALN/ Back in the 1980s, J.D.

Gartner found Christianity reduced the chances of admission to psychology doctoral programs. Using 1999 data, "The Still Divided Academy" by Stanley Rothman, April Kelly-Woessner, and Matthew Woessner offered strong statistical evidence that (typically religious) socially conservative professors must publish more to get the same academic posts. More recently, George Yancey's "Compromising Scholarship" showed that in many academic fields, significant numbers of professors, more than enough to blackball hiring decisions, express reluctance to hire evangelical and fundamentalist Christians.
33. 1 John 2:11
34. Dr. Myles Monroe, *Kingdom Principles*, 18-19.

THE SOCIAL GOSPEL

1. Teresa Morgan with John Dickson, *"Moral Classics," Undeceptions, season 1, episode 4*, 23 September 2019, http://undeceptions.com/podcast/moral-classics.

2. https://www.philanthropyroundtable.org/magazine/less-god-less-giving/
3. https://en.wikipedia.org/wiki/Women%27s_rights#cite_note-95
4. William Wilberforce, *Real Christianity.*
5. Martin Luther King, *Stride Toward Freedom*, 117.
6. https://learning.candid.org/resources/knowledge-base/number-of-nonprofits-in-the-u-s/
7. https://www.philanthropyroundtable.org/magazine/less-god-less-giving/
8. http://sectorsource.ca/research-and-impact/sector-impact#:~:text=There%20are%20over%20170%2C000%20charitable%20and%20nonprofit%20organizations%20in%20Canada.&text=85%2C000%20of%20these%20are%20registered,by%20the%20Canada%20Revenue%20Agency
9. https://brill.com/view/book/edcoll/9789004412927/BP000016.xml#:~:text=There%20are%20about%2030%2C000%20congregations,with%20attendances%20of%20over%201%2C000
10. https://www.philanthropyroundtable.org/magazine/less-god-less-giving/
11. https://en.wikipedia.org/wiki/Social_Gospel#cite_note-FOOTNOTERogersBlade1998181,_183-7
12. https://en.wikipedia.org/wiki/Social_Gospel
13. Matthew 6:10 (KJV)
14. https://en.wikipedia.org/wiki/Social_Gospel#cite_note-FOOTNOTERogersBlade1998181,_183-7
15. https://en.wikipedia.org/wiki/Social_Gospel#cite_note-FOOTNOTEAhlstrom1974White1990-4
16. Woods, Randall B., *LBJ: Architect of American Ambition*, (2006), 27, 430, 465–466, 486.
17. https://en.wikipedia.org/wiki/Social_Gospel#cite_note-FOOTNOTERogersBlade1998181,_183-7
18. Julian, *Fragment of a Letter to a Priest* 305b–d (Wright, Loeb Classical

Library 29), 337-339.
19. Julian, "To Arcacius, High Priest of Galatia," *Letter* 22.429C–431B (Wright, Loeb Classical Library 157), 67-73.
20. Luke 10:37
21. John 13:34
22. Acts 2:45
23. Acts 4:34-35

THE CITY WITHOUT A CHURCH

1. Hebrews 11:15-16
2. https://news.asu.edu/20210513-study-beliefs-about-afterlife-affect-sustainability-practices
3. https://kinginstitute.stanford.edu/king-papers/documents/dimensions-complete-life-sermon-dexter-avenue-baptist-church
4. https://kinginstitute.stanford.edu/king-papers/documents/dimensions-complete-life-sermon-dexter-avenue-baptist-church#fn10
5. Martin Luther King, *"The Three Dimensions of a Complete Life,"* 24 January 1954.
6. Psalm 139:14
7. https://kinginstitute.stanford.edu/king-papers/documents/dimensions-complete-life-sermon-dexter-avenue-baptist-church#fn18
8. Martin Luther King, *"The Three Dimensions of a Complete Life,"* 24 January 1954.
9. https://kinginstitute.stanford.edu/king-papers/documents/dimensions-complete-life-sermon-dexter-avenue-baptist-church#fn18
10. Genesis 2:18
11. Luke 10:27
12. Henry Drummond, *The City Without a Church*, 14.
13. Henry Drummond, *The City Without a Church*, 41.
14. Henry Drummond, *The City Without a Church,* 42-43.
15. https://www.livescience.com/christianity-denominations.html
16. Henry Drummond, *The City Without a Church,* 16.

17. Henry Drummond, *The City Without a Church,* 39-40.
18. Henry Drummond, *The City Without a Church,* 25.
19. Martin Luther King, "*The Three Dimensions of a Complete Life,*" 24 January 1954). King once attributed this illustration to Benjamin Mays (King, "Facing the Challenge of a New Age," Address Delivered at NAACP Emancipation Day Rally, 1 January 1957, in Papers, 4:79).
20. Henry Drummond, *The City Without a Church,* 20.

MY CITY CARE

1. Matthew 7:15
2. Matthew 25:21
3. John 13:15
4. 1 Corinthians 11:1
5. Luke 19:41
6. Henry Drummond, *The City Without a Church,* 16-17.
7. Gregory of Nazianzus, Third Theological Oration, in *On God and Christ,* trans. Frederick Williams and Lionel Wickman (Crestwood, NY: St. Vladimir's Seminary Press, 2002), 88.
8. Matthew 25:40
9. https://www.wikiwand.com/en/Charity_(Christian_virtue)#citenote10 ; Select Orations (translated by Martha Vinson)". www.jstor.org. Retrieved 2 January 2022.
10. https://www.wikiwand.com/en/Charity_(Christian_virtue)#citenote10 ; Select Orations (translated by Martha Vinson)". www.jstor.org. Retrieved 2 January 2022.
11. Robin Lane Fox, *Pagans and Christians,* (New York: Knopf, 1987), 324.
12. https://www.census.gov/newsroom/stories/poverty-awareness-month.html
13. https://cwp-csp.ca/poverty/just-the-facts/
14. https://policyadvice.net/insurance/insights/homelessness-statistics/

15. https://www150.statcan.gc.ca/n1/pub/82-003-x/2021001/article/00002-eng.htm
16. https://davidjoannes.com/shocking-stats-on-missions-giving/ Barrett and Johnson, 2001, 656
17. http://www.thetravelingteam.org/
18. https://davidjoannes.com/the-most-epic-monster-list-of-missionary-quotes-on-the-internet/
19. https://canadians.org/fn-water
20. https://www.dailyrecord.com/story/news/2021/02/12/liquid-church-cover-13-7-million-medical-debt-needy-nj-families/6736903002/
21. https://www.christianitynigeria.com/2021/12/liquid-church-set-to-distribute-11m.html
22. Henry Drummond, *The City Without a Church*, 54-55.

CONCLUSION

1. http://davidjoannes.com/the-most-epic-monster-list-of-missionary-quotes-on-the-internet/
2. Henry Drummond, *The City Without a Church*, 15.
3. Booth the Beloved (1949) by J. Evan Smith, pp. 122-124
4. Henry Drummond, *The City Without a Church*, 51.

Manufactured by Amazon.ca
Acheson, AB

32377682R00150